Crosscurrents / Modern Critiques / New Series

Edited by Harry T. Moore and Matthew J. Bruccoli

Thomas Pynchon

The Art of Allusion

By David Cowart

Southern Illinois University Press
Carbondale and Edwardsville

Feffer & Simons, Inc.
London and Amsterdam

Extracts used in the text as taken with permission from:
The book *V.* by Thomas Pynchon
Copyright © 1961, 1963 by Thomas Pynchon
J. B. Lippincott Company and Jonathan Cape Ltd.
The book *The Crying of Lot 49* by Thomas Pynchon
Copyright © 1965, 1966 by Thomas Pynchon
J. B. Lippincott Company and Jonathan Cape Ltd.
The book *Gravity's Rainbow* by Thomas Pynchon
Copyright © 1973 by Thomas Pynchon
All rights reserved
Viking Penguin Inc. and OBC and Jonathan Cape Ltd.

"Love and Death: Variations on a Theme in Pynchon's Early Fiction," *The Journal of Narrative Technique*, 7, No. 3 (Fall 1977), 157–69.
"Pynchon's *The Crying of Lot 49* and the Paintings of Remedios Varo," *Critique: Studies in Modern Fiction*, 18, No. 3 (1977), 19–26.
" 'Sacrificial Ape': King Kong and His Antitypes in *Gravity's Rainbow*," *Literature and Psychology*, 28, Nos. 3–4 (1978), 112–18.
"V. in Florence: Botticelli's *Birth of Venus* and the Metamorphosis of Victoria Wren," *Southern Humanities Review*, (Fall 1979).

Library of Congress Cataloging in Publication Data

Cowart, David, 1947-
    Thomas Pynchon's art of allusion.

    (Crosscurrents/modern critiques/new series)
    Bibliography: p.
    Includes index.
    1. Pynchon, Thomas—Criticism and interpretation.
2. Arts in literature   I. Title.
PS3566.Y55Z6   813'.5'4   79-20157
ISBN 0-8093-0944-0

This book is for Georgia

Contents

Acknowledgments

A number of people have contributed to this book. James McConkey and E. T. Cranch wrote from Cornell University with useful information about Pynchon's undergraduate days. People who knew Pynchon outside of academe—Whitney Bolton, Anne Cotton, and Walter Bailey—have also shared their recollections with me. In addition to checking the musicological references for accuracy, Georgia J. Cowart read and reread the manuscript, providing invariably sound criticism. Eugene G. Cowart, a mechanical engineer, checked some of the technical references. Matthew J. Bruccoli, David Leverenz, Andrew Welsh, Patricia Tobin, Richard Poirier, and Daniel F. Howard also read the manuscript, or part of it, offering comments which proved tremendously helpful. My greatest debt, however, is to Paul Fussell, whose encouragement kept my enthusiasm from flagging, and whose flawless critical sense saved me from many a gaffe and many an omission. These people are responsible for many of this book's virtues, and none of its flaws.

Thomas Pynchon

The Art of Allusion

1

Pynchon's Artistic Priorities

Thomas Pynchon impresses his readers as that rarity, the literary artist undaunted by science and technology. While many twentieth-century writers have had to contend with what one observer calls "the proliferation of things" in the modern world—an enterprise demanding at least some involvement with technology—few have done so with as much panache as the author of *V., The Crying of Lot 49,* and *Gravity's Rainbow.* In this respect Pynchon lies in the apostolic succession from James Joyce, who felt compelled to master in lucid prose not only the process by which thermal energy from the sun, stored for millenia as fossilized vegetable matter, eventually came to heat Leopold Bloom's shaving water, but also the process by which the water itself got from Dublin's reservoir to Bloom's tap. Joyce once described his mania for detail by saying that he had the mind of an assistant greengrocer. With a similarly all-embracing mind, Pynchon joins the staff of Joyce's implied world-grocery, with an even more formidable determination not to leave the higher or more remote shelves uninventoried.

Yet because of the scarcity of the Renaissance intellect in our time, Pynchon's mastery of science and his frequent, casual shifts into its language tend to impress us somewhat disproportionately. Such awe need not dismay, inasmuch as an interest in Pynchon's fiction may seduce readers not scientifically inclined into investigating subjects to which they thought themselves indifferent or hostile—into discovering, in other words, the contributions to human knowledge of James Clerk-Maxwell, Willard Gibbs, Rudolf Clausius, Hermann Helmholtz, Kekulé von Stradonitz, Max Planck, Werner Heisenberg. We must guard, however, against the notion that we can

1

"understand" Pynchon by studying thermodynamics, aromatic polymers, quantum mechanics, or any of the other subjects associated with these names—and applying the results of our investigations to the explication of the novels. By studying whaling we may become more able readers of *Moby-Dick*, but our ultimate appreciation of such a novel derives from much more than an acquaintance with or expertise in whatever craft, technology, or science the author may take as an aspect of his subject matter or setting. Perhaps the absence of specialized knowledge precludes full understanding of a novel, but such knowledge does not constitute a complete critical tool kit.

The most abused of these critical "keys" to Pynchon is the concept of entropy, a corollary to the second law of thermodynamics. According to this law, systems that produce work by the transfer of thermal energy cannot function at perfect efficiency; thus the perpetual motion machine does not exist for the simple reason that all engines run down. Entropy is the measure of inefficiency in such systems: the less efficient the engine, the higher the entropy. The literary mind would probably take little notice of such matters were it not for the fact that the world and the universe of which it is a part are themselves "systems" subject to entropy.

Literary treatment of this subject, however, does not begin with Pynchon. It has long been a staple of science fiction, from H. G. Wells's *The Time Machine* (1895) to Isaac Asimov's "The Last Question" (1956) and, less seriously, George Alec Effinger's *What Entropy Means to Me* (1972). Even Flaubert, earlier in the nineteenth century, saw literary possibilities in entropy. Among his notes for completing *Bouvard et Pécuchet* (1881) is the gnomic *"Fin du monde par la cessation du calorique."* Unfortunately, entropy caught up with Flaubert himself before he could finish the novel.

Pynchon differs from these writers in that, less interested in the running down of the world or the universe than in the running down of the civilization into which he was born, he uses entropy as a paradigm of the snowballing deterioration of the West. But unlike some of his characters and certain of his critics, Pynchon realizes that the concept of entropy can be applied to society *only by analogy*, and that, consequently, no "law" says that a society's decline must be irreversible. Indeed, civilizations do not decline perpetually, but rather wax and wane. For that matter, the second law of thermodynamics does not preclude one's replenishing the gasoline in an engine so that it does not run down; similarly, one might be able to arrest or reverse the decline of a seemingly moribund culture. Some such meliorism does in fact seem to movitate a few of Pynchon's characters—and, I would argue, Pynchon himself.

Though one does not read Pynchon or any other author to learn about bleak cosmic truths like entropy, one may go to literature—to Greek tragedy, to Shakespeare, to Hardy—for an aesthetic or human response to them. Science becomes fictive to the extent that an artist succeeds in dramatizing human participation in and response to its revelations. Thus Pynchon's critics, demonstrating that snippets of calculus and probability do not buffalo them, must not neglect to defend, on artistic grounds, the inclusion of such nontraditional material in fiction. One could argue that Pynchon's scientific allusions, being a shade self-conscious and ostentatious, are the weakest component of his work. Criticism must avoid contributing to the unconscious assumption—shared, I think, by many nontechnical readers—that Pynchon is more of a scientist than a novelist. He may well be a brilliant amateur of science, but he has devoted his professional life to mastery of the literary craft.

Moreover, he devoted more of his education to literature than to science, for he did not major in engineering in college, as more than one biographical sketch maintains. According to E. T. Cranch, Dean of the Cornell University College of Engineering, Pynchon spent only one year in engineering physics, from September 1953 to June 1954, after which he transferred to the college of arts and sciences.[1] James McConkey, his adviser when he eventually declared a major in English, recalls checking Pynchon's record to see if he had transferred out of Engineering because of academic difficulties and being pleased to discover that "his record in that field was one A after another."[2] Pynchon probably did not declare a major until the fall of 1957, when he returned from the two-year hitch in the Navy which intervened between his sophomore and junior years at college. In the service he met a professor of English named Whitney Bolton, who had been drafted on completion of his Ph.D. at Princeton. Bolton recalls his amazement, after taking the battery of intelligence tests administered to armed forces inductees, on learning not only that someone had outscored him in mathematical skills (no surprise)—but that the same eighteen-year-old[3] engineering dropout had outscored him in *verbal* skills.[4]

The enquirer into such matters comes closest to the truth when he recognizes in Pynchon the erudition and intellectual range of a polymath. Thus the point of the biographical gleanings adduced here is not to suggest that the scientific component of his work should be ignored (and certainly not to hint that the author is some kind of scientific poseur). On the contrary, I wish to suggest that, as Pynchon aspires to a Leonardesque command of all arts and all sciences, his critics must approach his work with a breadth, a catholicity, worthy of him. I ought to admit, however, that his book began as a reaction to what seemed to me erroneous assumptions in the first wave of critical response to Pynchon's work. The reader may still discover traces of a polemical tone that came to seem less and less warranted as Pynchon criticism matured. Superseded now is the view of Pynchon as a brooder on entropy and other themes of decay; his world picture begins to appear more complex and more optimistic than the bleak vision formerly imputed to him. Some critics even profess to find more or less orthodox Christian leanings in Pynchon—and not just in the obvious fascination with Calvinism. They go too far, I think, but they do not err in suggesting that Pynchon may in fact take a relatively sanguine view of things.

Pynchon could find encouragement for such a view in certain modern currents of both art and science. In an early draft of this study I insisted—always a bit uncomfortably—that Pynchon's scientific allusions were not particularly central or important; were in fact flaws, sophomoric self-indulgence. Pynchon's real interests, I felt, lay primarily in the arts, and the key to his artistry—his greatest success—lay in his oblique use of them in his books. This notion kept me writing with a good deal of polemical and missionary zeal, but the longer I read Pynchon, the more I realized that the only proper approach to his work must be eclectic—must at once concede the breadth of his learning and his interests and celebrate their many-faceted reflections in his stories and novels.

Pynchon's writing, then, embraces both science and the arts. He has, in Housman's phrase, shouldered the sky, set himself the task of responding to *everything* in the experience of modern man. In his response, Pynchon catalogues, indexes, registers every feature of modern history, however chaotic, fragmented, or seemingly meaningless. If he does not, in the end, master it all, he sets a formidable example of dauntlessness before the awesome modern diversity. He also hints at possibilities for unity beyond the ability of our prejudiced, materialist minds to perceive or even, perhaps, to imagine. This tendency may prove hard to countenance for many of his readers; nevertheless, viewing human consciousness as something not necessarily circumscribed by the entropic drift that dooms other

forms of energy, Pynchon insists on intimating prospects for some
kind of spiritual transcendence, such as that described by Wernher
von Braun: "Nature does not know extinction; all it knows is transformation. Everything science has taught me, and continues to teach
me, strengthens my belief in the continuity of our spiritual existence
after death."[5] The final irony of this, the epigraph to the first section
of *Gravity's Rainbow,* may be that we are to take it straight.

Mirroring the breadth of Pynchon's allusive range is the breadth
of his appeal. Critics occasionally worry that he is merely the product
of a type of literary criticism that thrives on allusive, obscurantist, or
otherwise "difficult" writers. The more recherché these are, the
more extensive is the critical industry that can be founded on their
works, as more and more professors get tenure by explicating them
in the proliferating and increasingly specialized journals. Some critics even worry that the Pynchon industry in particular is rapidly
becoming precisely the kind of bureaucracy anatomized with such
savage satire in *Gravity's Rainbow.* But as long as Pynchon has a
substantial readership outside of academe, the academicians pose no
threat to him—as they do, paradoxically, to the writer whose audience comprises them alone. Scholars can support, explain, and
clarify—all worthy activities—without compromising Pynchon's extraordinary relationship with the common reader. And yes, that
relationship exists, for one encounters Pynchon-reading house-
wives, medical students, piano teachers, librarians, and high-
schoolers. In Selma, Alabama, for example, there is a
stockbroker—a Rotarian, and perfectly unspoiled by English
studies—who has read every word Pynchon has published. Indeed, a
taste for Pynchon even turns up among the desiderata of those
ridiculous classified ads in *The New York Review of Books:* "Fiftyish
executive, attractive, vital, seeks meaningful rapport with twentyish
attractive free spirit to share interests in yoga, the theatre, blues, and
Pynchon. Send picture."

These readers are joined by the many extra-academic editors and
free-lancers who have, generally with enthusiasm, reviewed each
succeeding novel for the periodicals in which important new fiction
receives attention. Still, one ought to concede that the average person will likely as not fail to recognize Pynchon's name if it comes up
in conversation and that Pynchon's most ardent admirers seem to be
concentrated in the universities, where they have generated an
impressive number of articles, dissertations, and books on this author's three novels. One very influential admirer is Richard Poirier,

whose scholarly work on Pynchon has appeared in *Partisan Review* and *Twentieth Century Literature,* and in his books, *The Performing Self* and *A World Elsewhere.* In addition, he has reviewed the novels, as they appeared, in *The New York Review of Books, The New York Times Book Review,* and *Saturday Review.* From the beginning, Poirier has expressed his conviction of Pynchon's greatness, and his judgment has been seconded by a majority of reviewers and critics, including Stanley Edgar Hyman, Robert Sklar, George Levine, Frank McConnell, and a continuously growing number of others. The tone of a review by W. T. Lhamon is typical: calling *Gravity's Rainbow* a "new milestone in fiction," he declares that it will "change the shape of fiction, if only because its genius will depress all competitors."[6]

The dissenters to this approbation have been isolated voices, often, I think, simply reacting to the bandwagon effect of Pynchon's popularity, which after a point tends to generate a certain resistance, if not to preclude dispassionate evaluation altogether. One reviewer argued that *V.* read like a collection of undergraduate creative writing exercises,[7] and Irving Feldman deplored, among other things, the author's sense of humor, "with its fatiguing brightness, its bad jokes, and toneless prose."[8] Subsequently, as Pynchon's reputation has grown, a rather small percentage of critics have written truly negative reviews. Representative of these would be "A Dissent on Pynchon," in which David Thorburn describes *Gravity's Rainbow* as "brilliant in parts but confused and exceedingly tedious as a whole."[9]

But generally the negative reviews and references appear in out-of-the-way places, and none come from critics with the authority of Pynchon's champions: Paul Fussell, Tony Tanner, Richard Poirier, Frank Kermode. Moreover, the fact that the negative responses have not grown (they have, if anything, declined)—even in the face of the calculated affronts to literary decorum in *Gravity's Rainbow*—argues that Pynchon is almost universally perceived as a writer of the first magnitude, a genius who richly deserves the many comparisons with Joyce, Melville, Rabelais, and Cervantes. In other words, a growing number of critics would agree with Edward Mendelson, who believes that Pynchon "is the greatest living writer in the English-speaking world."[10] One need only consider the absence of such agreement over the stature of, say, Mailer, Barth, or Bellow, to cite some of Pynchon's more important contemporaries, to see how remarkable it is.

Recognition in the form of literary awards and prizes has also reflected Pynchon's growing stature. The William Faulkner Foundation awarded its prize for the best first novel of 1963 to *V.*, and the National Institute of Arts and Letters voted the Rosenthal Foundation Award to *The Crying of Lot 49* in 1966 and the Howells Medal, which Pynchon declined, to *Gravity's Rainbow* in 1975. Little is known about Pynchon's refusal of the last award, but it may have had something to do with the Pulitzer Prize fiasco of 1973. Although the Pulitzer judges voted the award to *Gravity's Rainbow* unanimously, a supervisory committee overruled them, denouncing the book as obscene. Yet Pynchon probably found this episode more gratifying than the attempted award of the Howells Medal, for an artist is in trouble if, obliged traditionally to shock the bourgeois, he suddenly finds the bourgeois lining up to do him honor.

In addition to literary prizes, reviews, and popular appeal, a living writer's reputation rests on the considered response of critics and scholars in articles and books produced without the pressure of review deadlines. The major critical approaches to Pynchon have only begun to be differentiated, for critics are still testing the efficacy of ways to write about his work. The one clear distinction would be between the first critical studies, which tended to emphasize themes of entropy and decline, and the second wave, which sees in Pynchon attempts to counter rather than propound the world view derived from the second law of thermodynamics. To a certain extent these two phases simply mirror Pynchon's own development from something like nihilism to something more speculative, and critics who have been with him from the beginning have often managed to adjust their readings of his work as he develops. Thus Joseph Slade, in his 1977 article, "Escaping Rationalization: Options for the Self in *Gravity's Rainbow*," follows up his pioneering study, *Thomas Pynchon* (1974), and argues that Pynchon seeks seriously to escape from the materialist cul-de-sac of Western rationalism and the ecology-destroying technologies it has fostered: "Like Jung, Pynchon lends a sympathetic ear to the claims of intuition and the occult."[11] By contrast, Tony Tanner, updating the discussion of *V.* and *The Crying of Lot 49* in his *City of Words* (1971), continues to see the entropy idea applied to cultures, civilizations, and the social fabric itself: "Pynchon is a genuine poet of decay and decline . . . of a world succumbing to an irreversible twilight of no-love, no human contact."[12]

If a first phase of Pynchon criticism can be isolated and located in print, it will be found, to a large extent, in the work of critics who have written a single early article and then moved on. Some of the articles have become "classics," enshrined in footnotes and *Twentieth*

Century Views, and they remain good introductions to certain basis ways of reading Pynchon. These are the studies that examine the influence on Pynchon of *The Education of Henry Adams* and *The White Goddess,*[13] or explicate the novels as meditations on entropy,[14] or, more profitably, consider Pynchon's conception of history.[15] But these seminal articles have been superseded by a criticism that attempts to deal with the Faustian anxiety that characterizes all of Pynchon's stories and novels and culminates in the myriad references to Kabbalism, magic, primitive ritual, and the occult generally in *Gravity's Rainbow.* An early and prophetic voice in this criticism is W. T. Lhamon, who recognized from the first an antithetical balance in Pynchon's work between entropy and some imminent Pentecostal revelation.[16] The critic who speaks most persuasively for Pynchon's tropism for spiritual alternatives, however, is Edward Mendelson, who has done the finest work on Pynchon to date—particularly in his essay, "The Sacred, the Profane, and *The Crying of Lot 49*" (1975), the argument of which stems from the pervasive presence in that novel of language associated with religion. Mendelson has written in a similar vein on *Gravity's Rainbow,* as has Mark Siegel, author of *Creative Paranoia* (1978). Siegel rightly takes to task the critics who applaud or deplore what they mistakenly take to be "apocalyptic nihilism" in the book. "Despite its frequent grimness," he writes, "this is not a novel of despair, but one of possibility."[17]

The present study seeks to augment and consolidate this trend in Pynchon criticism. It will also, by concentrating on Pynchon's interest in the arts, provide a needed counterweight to the numerous studies of Pynchon's use of science. Analyses of Pynchon's references to quantum mechanics, cybernetics, Heisenberg's uncertainty principle, abstruse mathematics, and thermodynamics have been accruing since the publication of *V.,* and the time has come to examine Pynchon's use of painting, film, music, and literature.

All of Pynchon's allusions—scientific and artistic—form patterns that lend unity not only to the individual stories and novels, but to the author's work as a whole. These patterns adumbrate an antinomy between the entropic, voidward drift implicit in a materialist view of things, and the possibilities for transcendence implicit in a spiritual view, and they do so whether one examines art or science in Pynchon. Thus to suggest that this antinomy corresponds to a dichotomy between science and art would be misleading, for in the mysteries of modern chemistry and physics Pynchon finds a good deal of latitude for an existential optimism to counter the spiritual bad news of decades and even centuries of materialist science. Similarly, the antinomy may be found in Pynchon's use of the arts: he limns a nihilist world picture with allusions from painting and film and a more speculative one with allusions from music and literature.

The two-dimensional pictorial arts furnish emblems of life's appalling insubstantiality. Botticelli's *Birth of Venus* in *V.* and Varo's *Bordando el Manto Terrestre* in *The Crying of Lot 49* teach their viewers something terrible about the human condition. Seeing these paintings, characters like Rafael Mantissa and Oedipa Maas experience the same chilling epiphany: life masks a Void. In *Gravity's Rainbow,* a book at once structured as a movie and filled with movie allusions, the two-dimensional emblem becomes kinetic. Here Pynchon argues life's substantial inferiority to its own aesthetic "projections," for throughout the book he demonstrates repeatedly that film can be every bit as real as life—that, indeed, life imitates the movies far more systematically than the other way around. But again, the ultimate message does not differ from that associated with the simpler pictorial allusions: beyond life lies nothing more substantial than a blank white screen, a Void.

The complement to this bleak picture comes in the musical and literary allusions. The musical references seem always to hint at the extra dimensions of experience that we miss because of the narrow range of frequencies—physical or spiritual—to which we are attuned. Thus Pynchon often refers to those serial and electronic composers who have forced music out of old patterns and sought to go beyond fixed musical scales. When Oedipa Maas hears the music of Stockhausen, for example, it signals that she will soon learn the inadequacy of certain perceptual habits, certain mental attitudes by which she has long been blinded to the hidden truth about her country and even about the phenomenal world. Similarly the music of Anton Webern becomes associated, in *Gravity's Rainbow,* with a world of anarchic choices—not only in composition, but also in politics, physics, and economics. Music in Pynchon, then, is associated with rich new possibilities beyond our normal powers of observation, with what the author calls "orders behind the visible" (*Gravity's Rainbow,* p. 188).

The majority of the literary allusions abet and extend the almost mystical tendency observed in the musical allusions. In E. M. Forster, in Rilke, in Lewis Carroll, and in the literary craft itself—particularly metaphor—Pynchon finds support for a surprisingly sanguine world picture. Moreover, the subtle use he makes of his reading demonstrates an acute sense, on his part, of what allusion can reasonably be expected to do. Traditionally an allusion makes the passage in which it occurs more cogent by its indirect appeal to "authority," or, providing some enrichment of context or increment of meaning, it makes a small contribution to that density which is such an important attribute of literary language.

It can also provide a shortcut to meaning, though the proposed shortcut may prove a cul-de-sac if understanding a passage depends on recognizing an allusion. Excluding the allusive practice of a writer like Ezra Pound, who often intended his arcane references to function didactically (forcing his reader to learn economic history or the classics), one can say that an allusion ought properly to function as an accent or grace note, not a cynosure. References as likely to impede as to assist understanding run counter to the spirit and purpose of allusion; indeed, some of Pynchon's scientific allusions may be reproached on just this score. When these are not set forth at self-explanatory length, they seem crucial to the sense of the passages in which they appear. Because they appear to squat in the path of meaning, and thus to take on what may be a deceptive prominence, such allusions tend to cause a certain amount of frustration in the reader; they may not sit well with those who expect indirection and understatement to be the stuff of artistry.

Just this subtlety, however, does characterize Pynchon's literary allusions, at least those in his native language. In contrast to the showy scientific allusions, these often appear so unobtrusively as to go unnoticed by any but the most attentive reader. When coal in the earth is described as swaddled "in layers of perpetual night" (*Gravity's Rainbow,* p. 166), the echo of Sir Thomas Browne ("But seeds themselves do lie in perpetual shades") has been attenuated to a single adjective and a context. Similarly, one cannot know for certain whether a reference to "that Other Kingdom" (*Gravity's Rainbow,* p. 722) is an allusion to the Forster short story of that title, or to the lines from Eliot's "The Hollow Men." And with only the iteration and a garden setting to support the attribution, one cannot declare unequivocally that a phrase as brief as "find them, find them."[18] comes to Pynchon from "Burnt Norton."

According to Joseph Slade, author of the first book-length study of Pynchon, T. S. Eliot was one of the earliest literary influences on the author. Slade shows how the early short stories, "Mortality and Mercy in Vienna" and "Lowlands," are almost meditations on *The Waste Land* and "The Hollow Men."[19] But by the writing of *V.,*

Pynchon had come to regard the Eliot influence with a certain irony. He makes Fausto Maijstral smile at the poet's influence on the Maltese literary "Generation of '37." The favorite poem of Fausto's circle is "The Hollow Men," though we learn more about what came of their interest in *Ash-Wednesday.* Fausto's friend Dnubietna writes a parody of the poem:

> Because I do
> Because I do not hope
> Because I do not hope to survive
> Injustice from the Palace, death from the air.
> Because I do,
> Only do,
> I continue. (p. 308)

Eliot's version turns continually on the idea of "turning again" to fleshly concerns. The poem is still in Pynchon's mind in *Gravity's Rainbow,* where Pirate Prentice reflects sadly that the woman he loved, Scorpia Mossmoon, is "lost to Pirate now for good, no chance for either of them to turn again" (p. 544). Here the allusion is closer to the fleshly theme of the original. We might doubt that this is even a deliberate allusion, were it not that Eliot had been associated with the Prentice-Mossmoon romance before. Scorpia had called the beginning of their affair in 1936 "a T. S. Eliot April" (p. 35).

While Pynchon can expect a fairly extensive literary knowledge on the part of his readers, he cannot assume the same level of sophistication with regard to music; consequently, musical allusion figures less obliquely in his fiction. One of those polls which gauge every fluctuation of American taste and preference recently revealed that music now precedes sex in order of importance to the young American male. Pynchon has not yet come to that pass, but music does seem more important to him as he gets older, for the density of musical allusion in his writing increases as his career progresses. From his first published story to his last, Pynchon's short fiction continually features sophisticated use of musical allusion. The protagonist of "Mortality and Mercy in Vienna" (1959), for example, defines himself and his surroundings in terms of his reponses to the *Concerto for Orchestra* and *Faust,* while in "Lowlands" (1960) Pig Bodine and a trash collector named Rocco Squarcione join Dennis Flange to swill wine and listen to Vivaldi. In "Entropy" (1960) pot-smoking party guests raptly enjoy "The Great Gate of Kiev," and in "Under the Rose" (1961) an infrastructure of references to Puccini's

Manon Lescaut provides ironic counterpoint to the story's action at every point. As for the longer fiction, *V.* teems with references to Stravinsky, Mozart, Wagner, Schönberg, Puccini, and Vivaldi, while in *The Crying of Lot 49* Oedipa Maas has Bartók on the inside of her head and Muzak-Vivaldi on the outside. But in *Gravity's Rainbow* the musical allusion comes into its own. The host of composers mentioned include Bach, Purcell, Beethoven, Verdi, Orff, Tallis, and Britten. Pynchon now ranges all of musical history for his allusions, from Anton Webern back to the legendary minnesinger Tannhäuser.

The *Tannhäuser* allusions provide a good example of how much music can contribute to Pynchon's fictional enterprise. The author seems to make of his character Tyrone Slothrop a modern Tannhäuser, questing hopelessly for some form of personal redemption. The *Tannhäuser* frame provides added significance in passages that at first glance appear nothing more than exuberant nonsense, e.g., the sequence in which Major Marvy and his "Mothers," singing dirty limericks, pursue Slothrop through the *Stollen*[20] under the mountain at Nordhausen. The scene elaborately burlesques *Tannhäuser*'s song contest on the theme of love. That all of the Mothers' songs celebrate a particularly decadent type of physical love is ironic, because singing of erotic love was the very gaffe committed by Tannhäuser in the Wartburg.

Pynchon scatters references to music through his fiction much more copiously than references to art. Though chiefly interested in the graphic arts, Pynchon does not ignore plastic art altogether: *V.* contains references to Cellini and Tagliacozzi, and "A Journey into the Mind of Watts," Pynchon's single venture into nonfiction, takes as its focal image a piece of junk sculpture, which Joseph Slade describes as "a metaphor for the wasted lives in the black ghetto."[21] But Pynchon exploits the arts more effectively in *V.* and *The Crying of Lot 49* with his allusions to the work of Botticelli and Remedios Varo. Each of these novels contains a brief but intensely rendered set piece of allusion in which a painting functions as an early guidepost to thematic clarity. In *Gravity's Rainbow,* which includes only desultory references to artists and their work, this device of the single resonant painting disappears, as abundant movie allusions provide an allusive presence for the graphic arts. Consequently, this study of Pynchon's art of allusion will begin with an examination of the significance of the Botticelli and Varo allusions in the first two novels and a consideration of the use of film in *Gravity's Rainbow,* before proceeding to more integral analyses of musical and literary allusion.

2

Surface and Void: Paintings in *V.* and *The Crying of Lot 49*

In *V.*, and again in *The Crying of Lot 49,* Pynchon introduces and describes a single painting, as if to provide his text with the prose equivalent of an "illustration" or emblem. In *The Crying of Lot 49* the author refracts through the eyes of his heroine, Oedipa Maas, a detailed description of Remedios Varo's little-known *Bordando el Manto Terrestre,* a painting whose solipsistic theme complements that of Pynchon's novel. Similarly, in *V.,* Botticelli's *Birth of Venus* functions as a kind of cultural touchstone by which readers may gauge the awful significance of another, more apocalyptic "birth"—that of V. herself.

V. consists of two separate but related narratives, one set in the present (the fifties), the other set in the half-century leading up to the present. Benny Profane, ex-sailor, road mender, night watchman, and self-proclaimed "schlemihl," bums his way up and down the Eastern Seaboard, the aimlessness of his wandering suggestive of a besetting modern anomie. Coming to rest briefly in the society of a group of effete pseudointellectuals known as the Whole Sick Crew, Profane meets Herbert Stencil, a man who has devoted himself to finding information about V., a mysterious woman whose dark and bloody career parallels the dark and bloody unfolding of the twentieth century. V. seems intimately involved with the century's violence and bloodshed, gravitating naturally to its wars and sieges, and Stencil has begun to believe that she is at the heart of some vast conspiracy behind the ills of the age. The "conspiracy," along with the illusion of V.'s agency as shaper or influencer of history, no doubt begins and ends in Stencil's paranoia, but the woman herself, the compelling symbol of a culture that has destroyed itself with violence and drifted into dissolution and triviality, cannot be dis-

13

missed so easily. V. personifies the forces that have sapped the vitality of modern men and made of them a "Sick Crew." She is figuratively the mother of this generation, as she is literally the mother of Herbert Stencil, and as we follow the course of her life through the investigations of her son, she seems less and less an ordinary flesh-and-blood woman and more and more the archetypal Terrible Mother of the mythographers.[1]

In the beginning, though, she was not terrible. As an ingenuous young Englishwoman named Victoria Wren, she was as fresh and lovely as the goddess in Botticelli's *Birth of Venus,* which figures briefly but importantly early in the novel. A crucial chapter, set in *fin de siècle* Florence, sees the commencement of Victoria Wren's transformation into V., and Pynchon's allusions to the Botticelli masterpiece make the painting an ironic emblem for the book's eponymous character at the inception of her decadent career.

The world has always recognized in the *Birth of Venus* a double perfection—the ideally beautiful representation of ideal beauty itself. Raphael Mantissa, an apparently free-lance political operative in Pynchon's imaginary Florence of 1899, admires the painting in a particularly intense way, seeking in a Renaissance work of art something he finds missing in his life, something transcendent or absolute. Mantissa belongs, the narrator observes, to a "circle . . . whose outer rim was tangent to rims enclosing the Decadents of England and France, the Generation of '98 in Spain, for whom the continent of Europe was like a gallery one is familiar with but long weary of" (p. 160). In other words, Mantissa's idealizing of a thing of beauty associates him with the cult of aestheticism. His eventual disillusionment may be associated with the discrediting of that movement. Though he treats Mantissa sympathetically, Pynchon's distrust of aestheticism comes out in the irreverence with which he refers to its chief apologists, Walter Pater and Oscar Wilde. The author strikes the Wildean note, for example, when he introduces young Evan Godolphin (who will later come to the same pass as Dorian Gray's picture) "sporting a costume too Esthetic for such a fat boy" (p. 156). And Wilde's mentor, Pater, turns up too: we learn that Evan "belonged to a generation of young men who no longer called their fathers pater because of an understandable confusion with the author of *The Renaissance*" (p. 157).

Pynchon seems to have consulted Pater in creating the character of his Botticelli admirer, Signor Mantissa, for in *The Renaissance* Pater describes the Florentine painter's work in terms that correspond to those Pynchon employs in evoking the sad little agent's personality. The most prominent characteristic of the painting Mantissa so idealizes is, according to Pater, its air of melancholy. Botticelli painted "men and women . . . saddened perpetually by the shadow upon them of the great things from which they shrink." Of the *Birth of Venus* he says: "What is unmistakeable is the sadness with which he has conceived the goddess of pleasure, as the depositary of a great power over the lives of men."[2] Pynchon makes this same melancholy the most prominent trait of Signor Mantissa. His eyes reveal "a free-floating sadness," and if one "kept watching long enough the plasma behind those eyes would soon run through every fashionable permutation of grief," so that one would have the impression of attending "a street-long festival of sorrow with no booth the same, no exhibit offering anything solid enough to merit lingering at" (p. 160). Mantissa's is a melancholy born of years of fruitless political idealism which he caps with a grandly futile attempt to realize another kind of ideal—an aesthetic one. Obsessed with Botticelli's masterpiece, he plans to steal it with the aid of two assistants: his sidekick Cesare and a bold, ambivalent figure known as "The Gaucho," an ostensibly Latin American revolutionary agent.

This Gaucho merits closer examination, for he not only participates in the plot to steal the Botticelli, but also functions as a Conradian "psychological double" of Victoria Wren, the character on whom the painting has the most obvious bearing. In Florence to organize a demonstration to embarrass the Venezuelan consulate, the Gaucho readily falls in with Mantissa's plot, as it will provide a useful diversion on the night of his planned march. Pynchon intimates that the Gaucho is using Signor Mantissa as the "makeweight" that the latter's name, in Latin, suggests he is. That the name has such a meaning in the language of the Caesars reveals Pynchon's irony, for Mantissa comes to be representative of the fate of his melancholy nation, reduced to makeweight status in two world wars—and almost the Germans' makeweight in both.

Though the Gaucho has some winning qualities, he is certainly no art fancier, seeing in Botticelli's painting only a nude to leer at. Venus looks "fat and blond, and the Gaucho, being a tedesco in spirit, appreciated this" (p. 178). Nor is his philistinism the only suspicious thing about him, for he is also an instigator of violence. His praise of liberty sounds occasionlly like cant, and when his demonstration comes off, he speaks contemptuously of the mob he leads: "Don't they look like apes, now, fighting for a female? Even if the female is named liberty" (p. 211). Like the genocidal German troops in South-West Africa, and like Victoria Wren's aborigine-suppressing uncle in Australia, he wears a wideawake hat. And while all the spies in Florence are on the lookout for German activity (the chapter illustrates the grandly muddled character of international relations in the years leading up to World War I), they overlook the only truly German element in the situation—the Gaucho's vaunted "tedesco" blood. As the Venezuelan vice-consul notes, trying to talk his chief, and himself, out of seeing trouble, gauchos are supposed to be from Argentina. Pynchon means for us to think of the country's reputation for harboring unsavory German émigrés.

The Gaucho evidently whips up unrest for reasons less blameless than liberty and enfranchisement for all. As with many professional revolutionaries—the insight comes from Conrad—the persuasive rhetoric and the captivating panache mask totalitarian proclivities. But the character of this revolutionary is more subtly realized than that of, say, Peter Ivanovitch in *Under Western Eyes,* whom Conrad never allows us to find appealing. The Gaucho's bluff heartiness is seductive; we hardly wonder that anyone could be taken in by his meretricious appeal because we are ourselves taken in to some extent. Nevertheless, we sense that although the Gaucho wears the Garibaldian red shirt here, he will change it for a black shirt within a couple of decades. When he cites with approval Machiavelli's call for "a lion, an embodiment of power, to arise in Italy and run all foxes to earth forever" (p. 163), we know that he will respond positively to the advent of Mussolini.

While each of the six "historical" chapters of *V.* pertains ultimately to the rise of fascism and the coming of the 1939–45 war, all but the two set in Malta pertain more immediately to the war of 1914–18, whose ill-managed peace set in motion the ugly political currents that eventually brought on the century's subsequent, more terrible global conflict. The Florentine episode proves no exception to this historicity; the Gaucho's demonstration, that set piece of confused international violence, prefigures the larger exercise in confused international violence everywhere expected in the chapter. Serving as backdrop to the Gaucho's machinations, the frantic international maneuvering in Florence, like the activities of the spies of various nationalities during the Fashoda Crisis in Egypt a few months earlier, typifies the kind of false labor the world suffered repeatedly before bringing the Great War to parturition in 1914. The Gaucho, like Gavrilo Princip, may be acting out of individual patriotism, but his act, like the assassination of the Archduke Francis Ferdinand, has the potential of precipitating the war. Although World War I does not begin in Florence in 1899, something else, its hour come round at last, does. Victoria Wren had been a study in ingenuousness in Cairo and Alexandria the previous year, but now, a confirmed demimondaine, she begins her existence as one of those feminine archetypes of the kind central to the historical and cultural theories of Henry Adams and Robert Graves. Adams, noting how the Virgin Mary inspired twelfth-century human endeavor, wondered what entity could articulate or unify the aspirations of modern man. Graves, on the other hand posits the White Goddess, a kind of Ur or matrix deity whose multitudinous and locally varied avatars include both the Virgin and the goddess Venus. The White Goddess, Graves argues, is in her various manifestations the mythic linchpin of the achievement of Western civilization for thousands of years. But as Roger Henkle observes in his succinct discussion of Graves's influence on *V.*, "Pynchon amuses himself by working into his fiction parodies of cultural and historical theories."[3] Pynchon implies that the modern version of any mythic feminine principle of the Graves or Adams type must be evil: no Virgin but a Great Whore—a goddess not of pleasure and love but of violence, death, mutilation, and perversion. Consequently, he creates a paphian Virgin, as it were—a composite figure who travesties at once Cupid's mother and Christ's. The previous chapter, set in Cairo and Alexandria, saw the deflowering of the Virgin; now, in Florence, Victoria Wren appears in the guise of a Venus, but one at the point of transformation into a chthonian being that thrives on pain and strife.

An elemental force to the ancients, Venus represented sensuality, the pleasures of the flesh, love, and feminine beauty. But the world has aged now, and so have its myths. Perhaps we are to understand that there was never any truth at all to the myth—that it was always a kind of Nazi Venus, a nightmare version of the eternal feminine, that we worshiped. More likely, however, Pynchon means to distinguish the modern era from the past in this regard. He introduces an apparent incarnation of Venus, then allows her to become distorted into something better suited to the twentieth century. His goddess, then, undergoes a chrysalis phase as the young, beautiful, and strangely religious Victoria Wren. But what emerges from the cocoon is, like Thomas Mann's *Hetaera esmeralda,* a creature of darkness and horror.

Why, we may ask, does Pynchon set Victoria's metamorphosis in Florence? He does so partly because of the opportunities for parody and resonance which the presence in the city of Botticelli's *Birth of Venus* affords. In more general terms he does so because, as a vast museum of Western culture, Florence provides an ironic environment for the pupal stage of the being that will embody that culture's decadence. That this being takes lessons in amorality from the book of a Florentine of the Renaissance compounds the irony. And though several characters in the Florentine episode operate "on the strength of a unique and private gloss on *The Prince*" (p. 199), Victoria, along with the Gaucho, embraces one of Machiavelli's most dangerous tenets: "She felt that skill or any virtú was a desirable and lovely thing purely for its own sake; and it became more effective the further divorced it was from moral intention" (p. 198). Virtú is the distinctive trait of any and every fascist strong man, and V. will admire its manifestations in D'Annunzio, Mussolini, and Hitler, who, practicing a statecraft unencumbered by any humanist ideal, would refine Victoria's understanding of Machiavellianism into the science of *Realpolitik*.

Herbert Stencil will later say, reflecting on the enigmatic woman who, in 1913, appears in Paris on the periphery of another prophetic riot, "Victoria was being gradually replaced by V.; something entirely different, for which the young century had as yet no name" (p. 410). Though Stencil should have moved the date of "replacement" back fourteen years to 1899, he identifies V. correctly: she is the fascist *Zeitgeist*. On her very first appearance in the Florentine episode Pynchon tells us that "she found herself acquiring political convictions, beginning to detest anarchists, the Fabian Society, even the Earl of Rosebery" (p. 166). Her subsequent politics may be deduced from a survey of the company she keeps in the years after Florence. She associates with the anti-Semitic Itague in Paris; with the Irredentist Sgherraccio; with the agitator for Italian sovereignty on Malta, Enrico Mizzi; with D'Annunzio in Fiume; with Bavarian Nazi Lieutenant Weissmann in the South-West African protectorate; and with Benito Mussolini in Italy.

Though we do not see her actually consorting with Hitler and Mussolini, they serve what she represents, and she is of their generation: V., 1880–1943; Mussolini, 1883–1945; Hitler, 1889–1945. The inhabitants of Malta, among whom she passes her last days disguised as a priest, wonder about the sinister figure in their midst. "What was there about this priest to put him Outside; a radius along with leather-winged Lucifer, Hitler, Mussolini?" (p. 339). Her career culminates in the century's climacteric, World War II, the holocaust "whose etiology was also her own" (p. 387), and her death in 1943, ironically in a German air raid, coincides with the first faltering of the Axis war machine. Yet the death of V. is as problematic—at least in Stencil's eyes—as that of fascism; a cancer does not die absolutely until the host organism dies.

But surely this perverse entity is not to be seen in the girlish, still outwardly virginal Victoria Wren of 1899? Herbert Stencil would seem to agree by placing Victoria's metamorphosis into V. much later. But Stencil's dating merely illustrates his unreliability, for V-ness—the pun is Roger Henkle's—comes into being in Florence, not Paris. The birth of V-ness is conceived as a travesty of Botticelli's *Birth of Venus.* Whereas the goddess of love in Botticelli's painting is born in daylight out of the breezy Aegean, V. is born at night in the midst of tumult. As one of the most representative cultural totems of the civilization whose decline the advent of V. inaugurates, the *Birth of Venus* stands for all that is endangered by the new dispensation embodied in V.

Pynchon may have gotten the idea of using the *Birth of Venus* as ironic counterpoint to the introduction of his modern goddess from Robert Graves, who describes the painting as "an exact icon" of the White Goddess mythos. In describing the general iconography of sea-born goddesses, Graves includes a comb, symbolizing heartlessness, and a mirror, symbolizing vanity.[4] Victoria comes equipped with both. The comb, a carving of five crucified English soldiers, is a grisly memento of the Mahdist wars; it is invoked, appropriately, as she impassively views the Gaucho's bloody demonstration. "From her hair the hands of five crucified also looked on, no more expressive than she" (p. 209). Pynchon provides his heroine with her mirror—many mirrors, actually—in chapter fourteen, "V. in Love." There the thing symbolized is nothing so harmless as vanity, but rather the inversion of lesbian narcissism. A final iconographic detail, not sanctioned by Graves, may be intended by the author's having Victoria often attended by Hugh or Evan Godolphin. Their surname puns on the name of the aquatic mammal that attends the goddess in certain ancient representations, e.g., the Aphrodite of Cyrene.[5]

Venus, according to Chaucer, "loveth ryot and dispense," but V. loves "ryot" primarily in its modern sense, for her transformation commences as she thrills to the Goya-like scene of carnage at the

Venezuelan consulate. "It was as if she saw herself embodying a feminine principle, acting as complement to all this bursting, explosive male energy" (p. 209). The riot is the birth, really, of Anti-Venus, the modern perversion of the goddess who so serenely reigns on the "western wall" of the museum that is human civilization. Importantly, riot and birth occur *pari passu* with the attempted art theft, during which Mantissa's accomplice Cesare slashes Botticelli's canvas to facilitate its removal, and Mantissa himself experiences his sudden epiphany of the void behind the painting's "gorgeous surface" (p. 209). The abruptness of Mantissa's perception is at least partially due to a kind of clairvoyant understanding, on his part, of what has just come into being a few blocks away, superseding the ideal of beauty and melancholy gentleness he has adored. We know that Mantissa's powers include this kind of preternatural awareness because Pynchon describes him as a member of "that inner circle of deracinated seers whose eyesight was clouded over only by occasional tears" (p. 160). Indeed, clairvoyance is hinted at in his name, for while *mantissa* is Latin for *makeweight, mantis* is Greek for *seer*.

Yet notwithstanding his clairvoyance, Mantissa's epiphany is in the first instance prompted by his friend Hugh Godolphin's account of a place called Vheissu, a strange, remote country of James Hiltonish romance and horror to which the Englishman, an explorer, had once led a doomed expedition. A land of surfaces, a land without heart or soul, Vheissu lingers in the memory as a play of shimmering, gaudy colors. It is an emblem of life itself, colorful and diverse, but ultimately without substance. Though haunted unspeakably by the place, Godolphin had not understood its full, terrible import until he had capped the Vheissu expedition with a journey to the South Pole.

The Antarctic, redolent of absolute loneliness and emptiness, is a recurrent symbol in Pynchon's works. Fascinated with the concept of entropy and the idea of a cosmic heat-death, Pynchon sees in the coldest place in the world an earnest of things to come. Godolphin goes there looking for answers; for him it is "one of the two motionless places on this gyrating world . . . the dead center of the carousel." (p. 205). A familiar conceit, this actually locates what T. S. Eliot calls, after St. John of the Cross, "the still point of the turning world." But where Eliot and St. John imagine an unmoved mover (Love), Hugh Godolphin finds only a token of nothingness:

> "What did you see?" asked Signor Mantissa, learning forward.

"Nothing," Godolphin whispered. "It was Nothing I saw."
(p. 204)

Reaching the pole alone, he had found under the pack ice[6] a Vheis-
suvian spider monkey's frozen carcass, planted there as a cruel joke
by the fiendish inhabitants of Vheissu, who have stalked him since
his escape from their country. In that desolate place old Godolphin
understands that Vheissu stands for "what the Antarctic in this
world is closest to: a dream of annihilation" (p. 206). The ultimate
nihilist vision, Vheissu teaches Godolphin that nothingness under-
lies all, that all life is merely cosmetics for the void. This knowledge
fatally afflicts his character; in later years his morals deteriorate as
his awareness of the groundlessness of all values eats away at his
innate decency like an acid.

In Florence we see old Godolphin as a Coleridgean figure. Like
the Ancient Mariner, himself the survivor of a terrible experience at
the South Pole, Godolphin feels a "compulsion to beg shrift of any
random passerby" (p. 182). He has become a wistful prophet of the
revelation he has experienced, preaching to his son Evan, to Signor
Mantissa, and, perhaps most fatefully, to a still relatively innocent
Victoria Wren. Thus like John the Baptist he has an early brush with
the incarnation of the gospel he proclaims. And as John, deferring
to Jesus, helped impel Him to His calling, perhaps the tale Godolphin tells Victoria helps her to hers. Whether or not Victoria's
development is influenced by the tale she hears from this old man,
his own development is clearly influenced—adversely—by contact
with her, particularly when he reenters her sinister orbit at Foppl's
siege party in South-West Africa in 1922. Godolphin's utter corrup-
tion is consummated then, as she teaches him what seems the great
lesson of South-West Africa: the conscienceless infliction of pain.

Godolphin is not the only character who might regret knowing
this woman, for very few of the book's innocent or decent characters
who come into contact with V. come away unscathed. Her influence
is almost invariably blighting: she inadvertently but fatally distracts
Porpentine the spy, nearly convinces Elena Xemxi to have an abor-
tion (she is carrying Paola Maijstral), seduces Mélanie
L'Heuremaudit, and makes the war-maimed Evan Godolphin her
creature. The last is another initiate of the Vheissu mystery, and his
youthful leadership of "a Nihilist group called the League of the Red
Sunrise"[7] (p. 157) is ironic in view of the basic, apolitical nihilism that
Vheissu represents. His gargoyle's face, being half-inanimate, marks
him particularly as one of V.'s own, for V. herself gradually incorpo-

rates bits of nonliving matter—false eye, false foot, false hair, false teeth, false navel—into her body. In converting herself by degrees into something inanimate, V. imitates and comes to personify the voidward drift of all life into a wholly inanimate condition.

V. and Vheissu, then, are aspects of the same nihilist truth, and the serenity of anyone acquainted with both is doubly jeopardized. Having just been introduced to both in a cafe, Signor Mantissa proceeds to his long-anticipated assignation with Venus unaware that his prospects of fulfillment are dwindling as a new knowledge and a new influence mature insidiously within him. Thus at the moment V. is "born" in the riot, which as we have seen occurs simultaneously with the raid on the Uffizi, Mantissa's beau ideal is debased: transmogrified into the vehicle of a terrible epiphany. The debasement of the painting is multiple: its subject (Venus) is displaced, its action (a birth) is travestied—and its status as aesthetic totem is deprived of power to comfort the sad anarchist's weary soul.

Art aspires to permanence, but even unaging monuments of intellect cannot long defy the underlying nothingness. At the moment when beauty can be his, Mantissa recalls old Godolphin's tale of Vheissu's shimmering colors, the gaudy mask of Nothing. In that moment he realizes that Botticelli's splendid painting is itself merely a "gorgeous surface" and that the goddess herself is only "a gaudy dream, a dream of annihilation." The blow is a terrible one, for she is "Rafael Mantissa's entire love" (p. 210). In an age in which man is denied all certainty, when his most cherished ideals and beliefs have become discredited, Mantissa had sought to provide himself with a substitute for these things and thus had in a small way fallen into the art-as-surrogate-for-religion fallacy so common to his day.

An effete later generation, that of the Sick Crew populating the novel's present, will be incapable of anything so nobly misguided. Art, for the Crew, means "Catatonic Expressionism" and paintings of cheese danishes; hence they know Botticelli only as a game whose object is the guessing of those proper nouns that constitute the whole substance of their conversation. And the goddess that Botticelli celebrated in his art survives amidst casual couplings and abortions only as something called Heroic Love. The Crew's vitiation is that of Western man in his twilight phase, drifting toward the final dissolution—the void—that V. had heralded. And Signor Mantissa was this Waste Land's Tiresias, knowing and foresuffering all in that single, intense moment in the Uffizi.

Mantissa's terrible epiphany is reenacted in Pynchon's second novel. Set in southern California, *The Crying of Lot 49* introduces Oedipa Maas, a mildly neurotic housewife whose sanity, no stronger than that of any other southern Californian, becomes further imperiled on the day she learns that she has been designated "executrix" of the will left by her former lover, a recently deceased millionaire named Pierce Inverarity. Attempting to disentangle the legacy with the aid of an attorney, Oedipa discovers that it reaches, by design or accident, into a startling number of crannies in the unsmooth facade of American society. Each part of the dead man's estate that she looks into leads her to some odd new substratum, underground, or glum assemblage of the American Dream's insomniacs. Never having known the extent of the alienation in her native country, Oedipa is distressed by what she sees, but she is more distressed when she starts to notice that all the undergrounds and subcultures are subsumed by what appears to be a master cabal, a bizarre communications system called Tristero. Originally an independent mail service, Tristero has for centuries, in both Europe and America, subverted, terrorized, and warred on legally established postal monopolies. By the time Oedipa happens onto it, it has gone to earth in California, still awaiting the opportunity to establish its legitimacy and meanwhile extending its tentacles into all the local pockets of disaffection. Thus Oedipa keeps finding new links in Tristero's network: her former lover, her husband, casual acquaintances, derelicts, Jacobean playwrights, Little Theatre directors—all seem to be part of it in some way. And one outlandish organization after another—from AC/DC, the Alameda County Death Cult, to Inamorati Anonymous—proves to be operating under the aegis of Tristero's logo, a muted posthorn. Where at first she wonders what undergrounds belong to Tristero, she eventually wonders what undergrounds do not. The harder she tries to get to the bottom of the mystery, the more involuted it becomes. Like a scientist stumbling on a problem of scarcely suspected complexity, she finds that the more data she masters, the less understanding she achieves. She begins to suspect that her own mind is the ganglion of Tristero's apparently endless reticulation; unless someone is playing an incredibly elaborate joke on her, she must be mad.

Pynchon refuses to solve the fantastic mystery he constructs. His artifice, moreover, is such that the reader, desperate for a resolution, begins to share Oedipa's frustration. Pynchon does intimate, however, that the ability to perceive unexpected diversity, even if one does so only through paranoia, is preferable to "the exitlessness

... the absence of surprise to life, that harrows the head of everybody American you know."[8] He shows us one woman discovering that life can contain surprise—terrifying surprise, perhaps, but still better than the drab predictability that denies the modern world a spiritual dimension.

The possibility of surprise ought to hearten anyone who, like Hugh Godolphin and Signor Mantissa in *V.*, becomes acquainted with the void that mocks all human ideals and aspirations. In a flashback early in *The Crying of Lot 49*, Oedipa, too, in an epiphany remarkably like that of Signor Mantissa, views a painting and discovers the void. Indeed, the painting, which she sees in the company of Pierce Inverarity, actually depicts the void over which life is spread like an inadequate tarpaulin:

> In Mexico City they somehow wandered into an exhibition of paintings by the beautiful Spanish exile Remedios Varo: in the central painting of a triptych, titled "Bordando el Manto Terrestre," were a number of frail girls with heart-shaped faces, huge eyes, spun-gold hair, prisoners in the top room of a circular tower, embroidering a kind of tapestry which spilled out the slit windows and into a void, seeking hopelessly to fill the void: for all the other buildings and creatures, all the waves, ships and forests of the earth were contained in this tapestry, and the tapestry was the world. (pp. 20–21)

The painting has a powerful effect on Oedipa because she has always seen herself as a Rapunzel imprisoned in a tower that is "everywhere." Pierce Inverarity, her would-be deliverer, cannot prevail against the tower's "magic," even when he translates her to Mexico. Thus Oedipa sees in the painting a representation of her own psychological-existential problems. She, too, is locked in a tower "like her ego only incidental" (p. 21), a tower in which she must embroider or spin out a world she finds uncongenial, even though it includes a trip to Mexico, a millionaire lover like Pierce Inverarity, and perhaps other lovers and other "trips."

The first thing to observe about the painting Oedipa sees is that it is not something Pynchon made up. Remedios Varo really was a Spanish exile who lived and worked in Mexico City until her death in 1963. Pynchon could have become familiar with Varo's work by attending any of the exhibitions of her paintings at Mexico City galleries from the late 1950's to 1964—one of the few things known about Pynchon is that he spends a good deal of time in Mexico. He might, for example, have attended the exhibition at Galería Juan Martín in June of 1962.[9] And perhaps he was one of the fifty thousand people who visited the giant Remedios Varo retrospective in the Palacio de Bellas Artes in 1964, the year after the artist's death. He seems to have been impressed with what he saw, and at some point he must have bought a catalogue or taken notes, possibly discovering in the fantastic, surreal Varo world a reflection of the world he was in the process of creating for Oedipa Maas. In fact Varo's iconography, and perhaps the information he would have picked up about her life, may have influenced the imagery and the theme of the novel he was writing. The case for such an influence will depend primarily on a detailed examination of Pynchon's two direct allusions to Varo, with emphasis on a thematic comparison between the triptych and *The Crying of Lot 49* as a whole, but the possibility of some indirect allusions may be considered first.

To read *The Crying of Lot 49* with a book of Varo reproductions at hand[10] is often to be struck by parallels in imagery and similarities of atmosphere, as if Pynchon had gone to school to Varo for his images. Frequently, for example, figures in Varo paintings materialize eerily out of tabletops and chairbacks, and especially out of frayed and many-layered wallpaper. The paintings seem to illustrate the "flinders of luminescent gods . . . among the wallpaper's stained foliage" (p. 126) hallucinated, Oedipa imagines, by the delirious old sailor whom she comforts after her night adrift in San Francisco. But the most intriguing shared image is seen in a Varo painting entitled *Invocacion* (1963), in which several large, ghostly figures seem to materialize behind a little girl who holds an evidently necromantic posthorn. The painting's air of mystery is enhanced by the fact that the name of its owner has been suppressed in the catalogue *raisonné* included in the definitive *Remedios Varo*. Out of the ninety-four paintings and drawings reproduced in that volume, only seven are in the hands of collectors so apparently publicity-shy.

If the publicity-hating Pynchon does not own this painting he ought to, for it is the very epitome of his novel, whose heroine also finds herself in contact with a host of shadowy figures through the agency of a posthorn. Oedipa, however, has reason to doubt the empirical reality of her horn and all it connotes. In fact she doubts external reality altogether as a result of her epiphany before *Bordando el Manto Terrestre*. Because of its subject matter, this is a painting which Oedipa, already seeing herself as the imprisoned maiden of fairy lore, is predisposed to find arresting.

Oedipa is a mental Rapunzel, locked in the epistemological "tower" of herself, forever unsure that what she perceives coincides with what really is. Aware of her plight, she will later hesitate to "project a world" (p. 82) because the projectionist, like the embroiderer, produces not reality but illusion. What, then, to do? "Such a captive maiden," Pynchon explains, "many fall back on superstition," as she does if she ascribes her problems to "magic"; or "take up a useful hobby like embroidery," as the girls in the painting do; or "go mad," as she does, seemingly, toward the end of the novel; or "marry a disk jockey," as she does after the break-up with Pierce. "If the tower is everywhere and the knight of deliverance no proof against its magic, what else? (pp. 21–22). But none of these alternatives is really acceptable because all involve remaining in the solipsistic tower. Still, "one object behind her discovery of what she was to label the Tristero System," the narrator suggests, might be "to bring to an end her encapsulation in her tower" (p. 44). Thus Pierce's legacy is important because it may—in the parlance of the sixties—be a means of "raising her consciousness" so that she can in some sense escape from the tower at last.

To understand more clearly the possibilities for an end to Oedipa's "encapsulation," one should consider the manner in which Remedios Varo ended her own encapsulation, for the tower in *Bordando el Manto Terrestre* is from her own past. Nor is its appearance in that painting an isolated example: a symbolic tower or castle figures prominently in at least fourteen of her hundred or so canvases. A typical example of this motif may be seen in the comparatively early *La Torre* (1947). In this painting a slender tower is situated in the middle of a kind of moat, which in turn fills the top of yet another tower. In the moat is a diminutive sailing vessel manned by someone who appears to be a deliverer, for against the wall of the larger tower is a ladder which becomes a road in the distance. The little girl fleeing along this road is Remedios Varo, escaping her tower. Its recurrence in her work, however, suggests that true freedom continued problematic for her; perhaps, like Oedipa, she was always haunted by a personal vision of psychic immurement.

Juliana Gonzalez, one of the contributors to *Remedios Varo* and evidently one who knew the artist well, suggests that towers and castles were indeed Varo's personal symbols for both a state of mind and the circumscribed way of life that engendered it. Born into a hydraulic engineer's family in 1913, in Anglés, a small town in the Spanish province of Catalonia, Varo could not thrive in her native culture. She grew up feeling stifled, even though her father took the family with him on business trips all over Spain and North Africa. She felt herself constrained to perpetuate what Gonzalez describes as "an austere world with walls made of virtue." The tower in which one is made to embroider a traditional world mantle is Varo's visual metaphor for the life she led as a daughter of Spain. Hers was "a world of shadows, of fears, of age-old furniture, of mantles embroidered with a secular craft; a world in which improvisation was inadmissable so that all is conformable and predestined."[11] Remedios continued to embroider this traditional world-mantle until the Spanish civil war made flight imperative. Like Manuela, Major Marvy's Spanish whore in *Gravity's Rainbow,* she became a refugee from a conflict only Brigadier Pudding and his Domina Nocturna, in the same book, could find memorable. In Paris Varo met her own knight of deliverance, the surrealist poet Benjamin Peret,[12] with whom she settled in Mexico after fleeing the Nazis in 1942.

This biographical sequence is illustrated in Varo's triptych. The castle is seen in the left panel, *Hacia la Torre;* in the foreground are a group of uniformly dressed girls, all but one of whom appear mesmerized. These are the girls who embroider in the tower of the central panel. There is more to this central panel, incidentally, than Oedipa notices: in one of the folds of the extruded tapestry—out in the world, that is—lurks a tiny, shadowy figure. Varo identifies him as the lover of the unmesmerized girl. She, perhaps realizing that if all reality is embroidered then the tower itself must be embroidered, is engaged in embroidering her way out of the tower by means of a *trampa* (Varo's word; it means *trick* or *trapdoor*) in order to escape to her lover. She is successful, and they appear together in the right panel of the triptych, *La Huida,* presumably voyaging toward new realities, in another of Varo's fanciful sailing vessels.

Free at last of the tower's enforced conformity, the girl will in the future no doubt embroider her own untrammeled version of reality, a reality whose richness any Varo painting discovers. Varo's work, as well as the life it reflects and transmutes, is of interest to us because it casts light on the Rapunzel-like plight of Oedipa Maas, allowing us to gauge the prospects of a self-achieved end to her "encapsulation." Though Oedipa perceives her problem when she sees it illustrated in the central panel of the triptych, she feels she cannot solve it, and weeps to think her isolation impenetrable. Even if she followed the narrative of the triptych to its happy ending, she probably would not be cheered, for her tower cannot be left behind in her native coun-

try, and her knight of deliverance is powerless. She will, then, tend to
be somewhat fatalistic as the Tristero unfolds around her. Are not
hallucinations and delusions the next logical steps as her solipsism
intensifies? In view of Oedipa's associations with one Varo painting,
her fear that she is embroidering the more phantasmagoric aspects
of Pierce's legacy in her head will hardly be dissipated by her encounter with another one, a reproduction she sees in the heart of
Tristero country later in the novel.

Oedipa sees the unidentified reproduction in Berkeley, where she
spends the night in "a sprawling, many-leveled German-baroque
hotel" full of deaf-mutes attending a convention (certainly a surreal
situation). The reproduction hangs on the wall of the room in which
she passes a bad night. She sleeps fitfully, thinking there is something vaguely minatory in the mirror, and awakes in the morning
"sitting bolt upright, staring into the mirror at her own exhausted
face" (p. 101). The nature of this episode allows us to surmise that
the painting in the room is one entitled *Encuentro,* in which a woman
opens one of a number of small caskets in a room, only to find her
own face inside staring back at her. Of this painting the artist wrote:
"This poor woman, full of curiosity and hope at the opening of the
little casket encounters only herself; in the background, on the
shelves, there are more little caskets, and who knows if when she
opens them she will encounter anything new?"[13] Juliana Gonzalez
carries this further: "In *Encuentro,* Remedios meets Remedios . . .
she contemplates her own countenance in one of the little caskets . . .
Remedios alone, engrossed; the solitude of Narcissus. . . . Will the
other coffers contain new outlines of her abandonment and
helplessness?"[14]

Whether or not this is the painting Oedipa sees, the reference to
Varo at this point in the book serves to remind her that everything
she finds in San Narciso, Berkeley, and San Francisco may have been
woven in her tower—just as she wove "what she stood on . . . only by
accident known as Mexico" (p. 21) as she stood before the triptych.
The book's chief ambiguity is that for Oedipa (not to mention the
reader) there is always the possibility that "the languid, sinister
blooming of The Tristero" (p. 54) takes place only in her "sick,"
tower-bound mind.

What Oedipa does not perceive is that embroidering, which we all
do, is not necessarily bad. We are all, as Pater says, engaged in the
perpetual weaving and unweaving of ourselves. The question is only
how freely we do it. Are we forced, unawares, to weave or embroider

some approved version of reality? The Tristero may or may not exist, but whether delusion or discovery, it is Oedipa's salvation, the *trampa* she embroiders to escape a world of conventional and deadly reality for a world of richer personal reality. That the Tristero and the whole tapestry of *The Crying of Lot 49* are being embroidered in Oedipa's head hardly matters: the important consideration is that she is now becoming responsible for her own mental tapestry. Her drift further and further from mental conformity should not be construed as madness: she is rather in-same than insane.

Utlimately, the index of Oedipa's fundamental sanity lies in her uncovering of something that is a part of the Tristero, yet beyond the imputation of brain fever. She discovers America's disinherited—the disgruntled, disillusioned, disaffected, and down-and-out whose existence is usually never even suspected by middle-class citizens like herself, brainwashed by the jingoistic pieties of the fifties. In the sixties—and *The Crying of Lot 49* is quintessentially a sixties document—Oedipa is led to know that the American syllogism is somehow fallacious; its middle term—those poor, huddled masses supposedly succored by opportunity and freedom—is undistributed. Yet to the average middle-class eye, America presents a smooth surface affluence, outwardly undimpled by discontent or want. This spurious homogeneity is the American desideratum; hence the melting pot is a cherished national myth. To the extent that the dominant American society achieves a kind of prepackaged, assembly-line sameness it becomes increasingly cloistered itself—blind to the very existence of variants in the national reality. Homogeneity, however, is no more desirable in a culture than in a heat engine; in either case it reflects a loss of energy, i.e., high entropy. American society thus courts its own petty version of heat-death.

The existence of an unnoticed army of the in-same, then, may prove to be the country's salvation. Oedipa will be part of this army, one of the nonconforming, the differentiated, the ununiform, the disinherited who wait for their heterogeneity to be recognized for the valuable, counter-entropic thing it is. The painful end of Oedipa's encapsulation begins with the simultaneous discovery of the Tristero and the shadowy American pariah-state it subsumes. In a way Oedipa *is* America, discovering in those parlous sixties not only an alarming and hitherto unsuspected heterogeneity, but also the different-drummer ethic which is its complement.

There being something of the surreal about the sixties in

America—one recalls serried hordes of demonstrators, assassinations, space exploration, incredible violence at home and abroad—Thomas Pynchon's novelistic canvas of the decade is perforce surreal in its mood and technique. In this canvas, as in Varo's *Bordando el Manto Terrestre,* the plight of a Rapunzel-like young woman comes to reflect the paralysis of a whole culture. As *The Crying of Lot 49* shows, in Hamlet's phrase, "the very age and body of the time his form and pressure," it also demands a new national penetration into value, beauty, and reality comparable, *mutatis mutandis,* to the ethical, aesthetic, and epistemological insights reflected in Varo's triptych. And as the paintings of that obscure but brilliant "Spanish exile" provide enlightenment for Oedipa Maas, so *The Crying of Lot 49,* Oedipa's story, provides enlightenment for those of her fellow countrymen who share her bewilderment about America.

3

"Making the Unreal Reel": Film in *Gravity's Rainbow*

Pynchon's pictorial-allusive imagination, manifested in embryonic form in the first two novels, takes on a special importance in *Gravity's Rainbow*, where it gives rise to multiple references to and metaphors from the art of the cinema. These allusions are more prominent, hence of greater structural and thematic importance, than the Botticelli and Varo allusions of the previous novels. Characters in *V.* and *The Crying of Lot 49* discovered the basic thinness of life by looking at paintings. Their insight, into the illusory nature of reality, becomes more complex in *Gravity's Rainbow* because of the greater number of pictorial allusions in that book and because of the more lifelike, kinetic quality of the medium that furnishes them. Film's two-dimensionality is still emblematic of a superficiality in life itself, but now the interaction between that which is lived and that which is viewed is far more exciting and convoluted: as if the interplay between Oedipa Maas's education in what constitutes reality on the one hand, and Remedios Varo's pictorial representation of that reality and its relation to the individual mind on the other, were multiplied and refracted—as if *The Crying of Lot 49* were set entirely in an art museum: not "a gallery one is familiar with but long weary of" (*V.*, p. 160), but one "wandered into" (*The Crying of Lot 49*, p. 20), hence fresh and compelling to the eye and mind.

In each of the novels, to a greater or lesser extent, Pynchon concerns himself with the relationship between life and its two-dimensional imitation. If life is itself two-dimensional in a metaphysical sense—"cosmetics for the Void" was the nihilist formulation arrived at in the last chapter—can one regard it as more "real," more "true," than its pictorial counterfeit? The question presents itself most intriguingly when the "counterfeit" is film (which is so much more perceptibly lifelike than painting that the English called their first movie theatre "The Bioscope").[1] In *Gravity's Rainbow* Pynchon uses film as a critique of life, insisting that the one is not more or less real than the other.

The novel's plot concerns Tyrone Slothrop, an amorous American army lieutenant stationed in London during the rocket blitz in the last months of World War II. Allied Intelligence begins to take an interest in this Lothario when they discover that the pattern of his conquests seems to predict the pattern of V-2 hits in the city. An unscrupulous psychologist named Edward Pointsman, determined to fathom Slothrop's preternatural affinity with the rockets, engineers an elaborate scheme whose first phase is to give the unsuspecting Yank a crash course in all the rocket technology Allied intelligence has been able to gather. The second phase, presumably to introduce Slothrop into greater proximity to the rocket, perhaps by allowing him to go AWOL under close supervision, to see where he will lead those who are watching him, never goes into effect because Slothrop, sensing that he is being used, goes AWOL ahead of schedule. Before he can be found, the war ends, leaving him to wander among the human detritus of a shattered and stateless Germany, which Pynchon refers to simply as "the Zone." Slothrop becomes involved with counterfeiters, black marketeers, doperunners, Argentine anarchists, a troup of black Nazi commandos, refugees, gangsters, mad scientists, American, British, and Soviet intelligence operatives, and the entire population of a Baltic village, not to mention a disoriented rocket engineer, a boy searching for his lost pet lemming, a nymphet, a balloonist, a witch, an ex-actress, a manic film director, and a pig named Frieda.

Eventually realizing the strange connection between himself and the V-2 rocket, Slothrop undertakes a personal quest to find out more, particularly about a special rocket, the 00000, designed by a Nazi madman to inaugurate manned space flight—with an expendable astronaut. His quest is ultimately no more successful than the quests of Herbert Stencil and Oedipa Maas. His fate is even more problematic, for he begins simply to fade, to cease to be a real, tangible person.

The story operates on a number of levels: politically, it concerns the unscrupulous manipulation of the weak by the powerful; economically, the conspiratorial abuses of the multinational corporations that may have actually engendered the war; and mythically, sacrifices leading to neither fructification nor resurrection—though the possibility of something like transcendence or transformation is hinted at. For the purposes of this study, however, the more important aspect of meaning is the ontological one, for the story concerns the inadequacy of cause-and-effect models of the phenomenal world, and of cozy assumptions about the ultimate reality of that world. For Pynchon, the vehicle best suited to challenge conventional views about reality is film.

One notices immediately in *Gravity's Rainbow* the great number of references to real and imagined movies, actors, and directors. The profound knowledge of the cinema that Pynchon demonstrates makes plausible the report that he nearly began his professional writing career as a film critic for *Esquire*.[2] Counting roughly, I find allusions to twenty-five movies, nine directors, and at least forty-eight actors and actresses. Pynchon includes everyone from Merian C. Cooper, codirector of *King Kong,* to Rudolf Klein-Rogge, star of German silents in the twenties; movies cited range from *The White Zombie* to *A Tree Grows in Brooklyn.* If the book does nothing else, it documents—copiously—the tremendous influence movies had on the pretelevision generation. But film is more to the novel than a source of culturally rich allusion: it is its ostensible medium. *Gravity's Rainbow* purports to be a movie itself.

For those of us born since 1930 (Pynchon was born in 1937), the second world war exists almost exclusively as a film experience. We may have read a few books about it, but mostly we know it through newsreels, movies, and television documentaries like *The Twentieth Century* or *Victory at Sea.* Those who actually participated in the war may perceive it the same way, for in America and abroad movies were the preponderant source of popular entertainment before, during, and after the period of conflict. Such a pervasive cultural influence must naturally have influenced the way the war was perceived by soldier and civilian alike—just as it affects the way we look back on the war today.

Thus in addition to structuring his novel as a movie, Pynchon presents a narrator and characters who falter in their ability to distinguish between real life and movie life. When, for example, Slothrop's counterfeiting and dope-running friend Emil "Säure" Bummer informs him of Roosevelt's death, the American experiences an eerie moment in which he perceives the bombed-out city of Berlin as a tremendous movie set:

> Someone here is cleverly allowing for parallax, scaling, shadows all going the right way and lengthening with the

day—but no, Säure can't be real, no more than these dark-clothed extras waiting in queues for some hypothetical tram, some two slices of sausage (sure, sure), the dozen half-naked kids racing in and out of this burned tenement so amazingly detailed—They sure must have the budget all right. Look at this desolation, all built then hammered back into pieces, ranging from body size down to powder (please order by Gauge Number), as that well-remembered fragrance Noon in Berlin, essence of human decay, is puffed on the set by a hand, lying big as a flabby horse up some alley, pumping its giant atomizer. (p. 374)

Besides being disconcerted by the shocking news, Slothrop may still be suffering the effects of Säure's hallucinogenic hospitality, but his sometime paramour, Margherita von Erdmann, whose experience of this kind of delusion is more or less continual, has no such excuses:

When Greta hears shots out in the increasingly distant streets, she will think of the sound stages of her early career, and will take the explosions as cue calls for the titanic sets of her dreams to be smoothly clogged with a thousand extras: meek, herded by rifle shots, ascending and descending, arranged into patterns that will suit the Director's ideas of the picturesque—a river of faces, make up yellow and white-lipped for the limitations of the film stock of the time, sweating yellow migrations taken over and over again, fleeing nothing, escaping nowhere. (p. 446).

Erdmann enjoys drawing others, like her daughter Bianca, or the American deserter Slothrop, into her fantasies. One of her "scenes" with Slothrop illustrates how discomposing her illusions can be under certain circumstances. Having been tortured and raped in a movie entitled *Alpdrücken* ("Nightmare"), she wheedles him into reenacting with her, on the original set, one of the movie's characteristically brutal moments. Slothrop's "role" was originally played by an actor named Max Schlepzig, whose name the deserter happens, at the moment, to be carrying on a forged pass given him by Säure. When the two realize that their playacting has this added, unexpected dimension, Erdmann's delusions are reinforced, and Slothrop is introduced to new refinements of his own incipient paranoia. The reader, meanwhile, is subtly disoriented. Neither

Schlepzig nor Erdmann are real names, any more than "Grand Inquisitor" or "captive baroness" (their roles in *Alpdrücken*) are real identities. And the "real" act—the sado-masochistic encounter of Slothrop and Erdmann—is merely an *imitation* of an unreal, illusory act—the sado-masochistic encounter of Schlepzig and Erdmann in *Alpdrücken*—though, as we shall see, the supposedly illusory movie has effects and consequences that lend it the most thoroughgoing claims to being real. Reality, in this episode, is layered. By peeling back the layers, one can reach a bottom layer, but it too, the acting of the movie, is illusion. Peeling *this* layer is useless; one cannot hope to find something more real beneath this final layer, for beneath it is only—the Void.

In view of this confusing of film and life, we should not be surprised when the headquarters of Vaslav Tchitcherine, a Soviet agent competing with Slothrop for information about the 00000 rocket, turns out to be a movie studio, or when our hero encounters Mickey Rooney in Potsdam, where the activities of the powerful seem more in keeping with a Hollywood premiere than with an international peace conference. Ironically, the characters who see World War II as a movie may be closer to the truth than those who see it in conventionally more sober terms. One can discover more justification for their way of seeing things by reflecting that war is an enterprise that often shares a vocabulary with the movies. "Action," for example, is a word common to both sound stages and battlefields. Both war gamers and filmmakers operate from a "scenario." Often one reads of directors who are "martinets" or "generals," or of movies that "bomb." Stars and combat riflemen have "supporting" casts and troops, respectively, and "shooting" may be done with a camera as well as with a gun. A "theatre," finally, may be either a place to watch movies or a geographical subdivision of a war. The phrase "it's all theatre," introduced on the first page of *Gravity's Rainbow*, is repeated over and over again (pp. 3, 267, 302, 326, 521, 722, etc.), as if to circumvent the reader's common sense the way television commercials do, by reiteration and unconscious suggestion. If the term "theatre" is extended to an enterprise in which one can get killed, along with thirty-five to sixty million others, then the distinctions between "acting" and "action," between war and the movies, between real and reel—are beginning, at least, to fade and blur.

The obscuring of the distinction between real and reel, along with the double meaning of "shooting," is central to the charming little poem supposedly spoken by the heroine of Merian C. Cooper's *King Kong:* Fay Wray, herself an actress of the Erdmann variety, whose talent is to cringe appealingly before various forms of brutal terror. She says that when she was hanging, bound, "waiting for the night's one Shape to come," she was not thinking of Jack, the young man who had kissed her just before her capture by the natives, but rather of her "Director":

> I was thinking
> Of Denham—only him, with gun and camera
> Wisecracking in his best bum actor's way
> Through Darkest Earth, making the unreal reel
> By shooting at it, one way or the other. (p. 689)

The poem is of special importance because it addresses the problem of reality versus cinematic illusion in its delightful puns, which not only link martial and cinematic activities, but also hint at the magical ability of directors to make the unreal *real,* whether the "unreal" be construed as *King Kong*'s world of prehistoric monsters or *King Kong*'s medium—film itself.

In *Gravity's Rainbow* film is never merely an entertaining illusion. Always, it seems to be in the process of calling itself into three-dimensional existence, or otherwise proving itself capable of inter-relating with "real life." In fact, Pynchon implies that film and life constitute two complementary forms of reality and proposes a number of seemingly contradictory things about their relation. He intimates, for example, that life imitates film, because film *creates* reality in its own image. Film, therefore, ranks higher in the ontological scale than ordinary everyday reality; conversely, ordinary everyday reality must itself be essentially immaterial, no more substantial than the flickering images on a movie screen. Such propositions may baffle and perplex us, but Pynchon cares less about propounding a coherent metaphysics than about challenging and subverting materialist complacency. The plasticity of the real which he insists on in *Gravity's Rainbow* ultimately may lead back to the Void, but perhaps it can also be adduced as an argument for the existence of some higher, less obvious reality.

Given Pynchon's premises, we should expect him to regard the film director, cinema's ordering intelligence, as a personage of no small power and importance; thus like the makers of *King Kong,* Pynchon introduces a director—Gerhardt von Göll—into his action. Von Göll probably wields more power than anyone else in the Zone:

he is the one person who can deliver Slothrop from the mess he is in, whether by providing information about the sought-after rocket, or by securing him a discharge. In fact, as far as Slothrop is concerned, von Göll is part of the bureaucracy of power that seems always to be deciding whether he is to live or die, be happy or miserable. To the extent that he uses Slothrop for his own selfish ends, von Göll suspiciously resembles another "director," Dr. Pointsman.

The concept of such a director as Pointsman—a remote and powerful person who controls one's life—is one immediately congenial to a paranoid like Slothrop, who really is, for a time, Pointsman's marionette (as, in a way, he is forever the marionette of that other unscrupulous scientist, Laszlo Jamf, who experimented on him in infancy). Pointsman is also the director of a mental institution of sorts, the Abreaction Research Facility, of ARF wing of The White Visitation, a clearinghouse for all war-related psychological investigations. The relationship between Pointsman and Slothrop recalls that between Dr. Caligari and Francis, the main characters in Robert Wiene's *The Cabinet of Dr. Caligari*. Though mentioned only once, this film seems to brood over the world of *Gravity's Rainbow* the way it brooded over Germany between the wars, according to Siegfried Kracauer's *From Caligari to Hitler*. Dr. Caligari, it will be remembered, is portrayed as a figure of evil until the end of the film, where we discover that he is the director of an insane asylum and that Francis, through whose eyes we have seen him, is himself one of Caligari's patients. Pynchon's novel inverts Wiene's technique: we see from the beginning that the "doctor" is unscrupulous and that he is inducing or contriving the madness of the "patient."

The "directors" Pointsman and von Göll, then, have more than the titular similarity in common. At one point they even cooperate on a psycho-cinematic project called Operation Black Wing. Conceived at PISCES (Psychological Intelligence Schemes for Expediting Surrender), Operation Black Wing is designed to play on the racial fears of the enemy. To provide information about such fears, Slothrop—before his desertion—voluntarily goes "under light narcosis" in Pointsman's Abreaction Ward "to help illuminate racial problems in his own country" (p. 75). PISCES then has von Göll shoot footage of spurious black rocket troops, which is to be planted behind the lines, where its discovery by the Germans is expected to result in widespread disquiet, if not general panic. The scheme is not as farfetched as it sounds. In a propaganda film entitled *Sieg im Westen (Victory in the West)*, the Germans made a special point of depicting the racially mixed composition of Allied troops. Scenes showing black and white French troops fraternizing were, in Siegfried Kracauer's words, "intended to arouse race bias and deprecate French racial behavior."[3]

Unlike the makers of *Sieg im Westen,* who had plenty of genuine French colonial troops to photograph, von Göll has only one Zouave at his disposal. The rest of his *Schwarzkommando* are various members of Pointsman's staff in blackface. On completion of the project, however, "von Göll, with a straight face, proclaims it to be his greatest work," and Pynchon invents a critic to comment on the irony of the observation: " 'As things were to develop,' writes noted film critic Mitchell Prettyplace, 'one cannot argue much with his estimate, though for vastly different reasons than von Göll might have given or even from his peculiar vantage foreseen' " (p. 113). The irony lies in the subsequent discovery that the black rocket troops are *real*—a development the PISCES staffers seem inclined to explain thaumaturgically: "At PISCES it is widely believed that the Schwarzkommando have been summoned, in the way demons may be gathered in, called up to the light of day and earth by the now defunct Operation Black Wing" (pp. 275–76). Von Göll cheerfully takes full credit:

> Since discovering that Schwarzkommando are really in the Zone, leading real, paracinematic lives that have nothing to do with him or the phony Schwarzkommando footage he shot last winter in England for Operation Black Wing, Springer has been zooming around in a controlled ecstasy of megalomania. He is convinced that his film has somehow brought them into being. "It is my mission," he announces . . . with the profound humility that only a German movie director can summon, "to sow in the Zone seeds of reality. The historical moment demands this, and I can only be its servant. My images, somehow, have been chosen for incarnation." (p. 388)

Prettyplace's observation, and the conclusion of the staff at PISCES, shows us that von Göll's conviction that movies can call themselves into real life is something more than the megalomaniacal delusion it would seem if he were the only one to believe it.

Von Göll also directed *Alpdrücken,* and it, too., is a seed-sowing agent. An entire generation of Germans owes its existence to *Alpdrücken*—Margherita von Erdmann became pregnant during the making of the movie, and she is so erotic on the screen that a lot of other German women became pregnant as a result of their husbands' seeing it. After describing the mental state of a rocket engineer named Franz Pökler as he rushes home to play *Alpdrücken* with his wife, the narrator asks, "How many shadow-children would be fathered on Erdmann that night?" (p. 397). All of these "shadow-children," including Pökler's daughter Ilse, Erdmann's daughter Bianca, and a young soldier named Gottfried (doomed to be the first, unwilling astronaut), will share a single identity. Erdmann, meeting Gottfried, recognizes her daughter in him, as does her husband, Miklos Thanatz, who reflects "that the two children, Gottfried and Bianca, *are the same* (p. 672). And the narrator wonders: "Ilse, fathered on Greta Erdmann's silver and passive image, Bianca, conceived during the filming of the very scene that was in his thoughts as Pökler pumped in the fatal charge of sperm—how could they not be the same child?" (pp. 576–77). Erdmann likes to think that Bianca was fathered by Max Schlepzig, her costar in *Alpdrücken,* but she can hardly know, inasmuch as she conceived the child during a gang-rape. Moreover, Pynchon suggests that the list of Bianca's possible fathers must also include the collective masturbators in *Alpdrücken*'s audiences:

> Of all her putative fathers—Max Schlepzig and masked extras on one side of the moving film, Franz Pökler and certain other pairs of hands busy through trouser cloth, that *Alpdrücken* night, on the other—Bianca is closest . . . to you who came in blinding color, slouched alone in your own seat, never threatened along any rookwise row or diagonal all night, you whose interdiction from her mother's water-white love is absolute, you, alone, saying *sure I know them,* omitted, chuckling *count me in,* unable, thinking *probably some hooker . . .* She favors you, most of all. You'll never get to see her. So somebody has to tell you. (p. 472)

Film and life cross-fertilize each other here. Like the Operation Black Wing footage, *Alpdrücken* sows what von Göll calls "seeds of reality," but in the passage quoted above, seeds are also sown on *Alpdrücken.* The words with which Pynchon describes the film imply that it is an interface between two realms of being, neither of which is illusory. The actors and the audience are not "on the screen" and "in the theatre," respectively, but "on one side of the moving film," and "on the other"—existing on separate spatial and temporal planes.

Normally the filmic interface acts as an impermeable membrane, a hymen as it were, preventing the interfusion of the two planes. Such is the power of this pornographic movie, however, that the hymen is burst and a general insemination occurs. The idea of film as membrane or interface also figures in Pynchon's allusions to *King Kong,* a film in which moviegoers have always recognized something more than mere sensationalism. The giant ape's essential nobility ("he was a king and a god in the world that he knew") and his capacity for love make him a remarkably sympathetic monster, one closer to the pathetic creature given life by Dr. Frankenstein than to the host of malevolent creatures that have become staples of the Saturday afternoon matinee. Kong also resembles Dr. Frankenstein's monster in that his story invites symbolic interpretation. Critics have seen in Kong everything from the black race to the repressed libido—not to mention mythic figures as diverse as Christ and Lucifer. In *Gravity's Rainbow* Pynchon exploits a number of these interpretations, while satirizing—in Mitchell Prettyplace, author of the "definitive 18-volume study of *King Kong*" (p. 275)—the critics who come up with them. Pynchon touches several symbolic bases at once when he declares that in *King Kong* lies the filmic genesis of the *Schwarzkommando:* "The legend of the black scapeape we cast down like Lucifer from the tallest erection in the world has come, in the fullness of time, to generate its own children, running around inside Germany even now—the Schwarzkommando, whom Mitchell Prettyplace, even, could not anticipate" (p. 275).

Prettyplace, we recall, had appeared much earlier in the book to comment on another film putatively instrumental in calling the *Schwarzkommando* into being—Gerhardt von Göll's Operation Black Wing footage. "My images, somehow, have been chosen for incarnation," von Göll will boast to his first postwar client; he makes the vaunt to one Squalidozzi, leader of a band of Argentine anarchists who no doubt find the Zone's temporary statelessness attractive. Believing, after a fashion, in the power of the filmmaker, the anarchists want von Göll to film the Argentine national epic, *Martín Fierro,* because the publicity and the glorification of the gaucho ethos of freedom will help their cause. Von Göll, his ego and his imagination inflamed, figures he can do more than that: "What I can do for the Schwarzkommando I can do for your dream of pampas and sky" (p. 388). The Argentines make an interesting connection between von Göll's magic Hereros and themselves. Argentina and South-

West Africa have for millennia been separated by the continental drift, but von Göll, in the course of his professional career, will have touched them both, and thus will have reeffected, in a sense, the ancient synthesis of the continents.

As a result of his presumed summoning into life of black men, von Göll's interest in *Martín Fierro* centers particularly on the scene at the end of Part Two of the poem, in which Martín Fierro and the Negro, El Moreno, accompanying themselves with guitars, sing improvisational *payas* in a musical duel. Von Göll imagines filming the scene with

> the peculiar and slow-moving "Emulsion J," invented by Laszlo Jamf, which somehow was able, even under ordinary daylight, to render the human skin transparent to a depth of half a millimeter, revealing the face just beneath the surface. This emulsion was used extensively in von Göll's immortal *Alpdrücken.* . . . With Emulsion J. he could dig beneath the skin colors of the contestants, dissolve back and forth between J and ordinary stock, like sliding in and out of focus, or wipe—how he loved wipes! from one to the other in any number of clever ways. (pp. 387–88)

Again film is the means of assaulting our complacency about what appears, at first glance, to be reality. The surface reality at issue in this passage—skin color—is an important subject in *Gravity's Rainbow.* Pynchon is a sensitive observer of relations between the races,[4] and in the suggestive description of von Göll's fondness for "wipes" he means to remind us of the psychoanalytic theory that accounts for racial prejudice in terms of the negative attitudes toward excrement learned in infancy. PISCES staff member Edwin Treacle, "that most Freudian of psychical researchers" (p. 85), tries vainly to explain to his colleagues "that their feelings about blackness were tied to their feelings about shit, and feelings about shit to feelings about putrefaction and death" (p. 276). Even the goodwilled Slothrop evinces such "feelings"; providing information on "racial problems" for Operation Black Wing in the Abreaction Ward, where one releases and verbalizes repressed emotions, he relives a collegiate visit to the Roseland Ballroom in Boston's Roxbury district. He fantasizes his near sodomizing by black washroom attendants, his escape down the toilet, and his subsequent journey through the plumbing system, awash in fecal matter. Much later in the book Pynchon suggests in another washroom fantasy that Slothrop, now dressed as Fay Wray, has "a repressed desire to be sodomized, unimaginably, by a gigantic black ape" (p. 688).

Other characters share Slothrop's repressed attitudes towards blacks. The triple agent Katje Borgesius, another of Slothrop's paramours, suffers them less acutely, but even after she has become a sympathetic character by joining the Counterforce, a movement that springs up at the end of the war to resist the oppression and manipulation practiced by the unscrupulous powerful, she cannot overcome a certain fear and horror of the *Schwarzkommando,* whom she visits as a Counterforce envoy. But the Russian agent Tchitcherine provides the best example of this peculiar facet of racist irrationality. He spends much of his time in the Zone trying to kill a man named Enzian, not because he is the leader of the *Schwarzkommando,* but because he is Tchitcherine's halfbrother—and black. The unconscious anal component of Tchitcherine's violent emotions is discernible in his private thoughts. He "thinks of Enzian as . . . another *part* of him—a black version of something inside *himself.* A something he needs to . . . liquidate" (p. 499).

Before considering the relevance of the *King Kong* allusions to this racism of the unconscious, we should note how systematically Pynchon inverts the ancient, and insidiously racist, symbology that equates whiteness with virtue, and blackness with evil. As blackness tends to be vital in *Gravity's Rainbow,* Enzian and his fellow *Schwarzkommando* are presented positively—even though a faction, the Empty Ones, advocates racial suicide. As whiteness, on the other hand, tends to be deadly, the novel's most viciously sadistic character, the man who conceives and directs the 00000 rocket project, bears the name Weissmann, or "white man." His *nom de guerre,* Blicero, also signifies a deadly whiteness, for "Blicker" was "the nickname the early Germans gave to Death. They saw him white: bleaching and blankness. The name was later Latinized to 'Dominus Blicero.' Weissmann, enchanted, took it as his SS code name" (p. 322). (Perhaps Weissmann was influenced by the SS insignia, a skull.) Weissmann's catamite, the pale-skinned and pale-haired Gottfried, is also a study in whiteness, like the swan that turns into another Gottfried in *Lohengrin.*[5] Blicero even dresses him in white lace for the firing of the 00000 rocket. Other white motifs include "The White Visitation," one aspect of whose mission is to communicate with the dead, and the pale mushroom cloud over Hiroshima that brings death to tens of thousands. Pynchon describes the atom bomb as "a giant white cock, dangling in the sky straight downward out of a white pubic bush" (p. 693). The giant member dangles presumably in post-rape flaccidity, but paradoxically one gets the impression of a malevolent and deadly impotence, the kind that must resort to violence to compensate for the inability to possess sexually.

At times the book's chromatic dichotomy is applied ironically. Despite her youth and beauty, and Slothrop's attraction to her, the decadence and bleak destiny of Greta Erdmann's daughter Bianca are hinted at in her name (Italian for white). This kind of irony is even more insistent in the novel's many "*Schwarz*"-prefixes. For example, the *Schwarzgerät*—a German version of what English-speaking engineers, referring generically to any specialized piece of electronic equipment, call a "black box"—is the human component that makes the 00000 different from all other V-2's. Considering the true coloration of the *Schwarzgerät*, its naming is a piece of bitter irony on the part of Blicero, who knows well enough the beauty and vitality of blackness, having been Enzian's lover before Gottfried's.

Nevertheless, the book's color values are not rigidly schematic. Although Pynchon avoids as unsuitable certain Nazi black motifs that were available to him (the SS was called the *Schwarze Korps;* a plot against Hitler was the *Schwarze Kapelle*), occasionally he allows traditional black-white symbolism to intrude. Usually, however, it is invoked by unenlightened characters. Operation Black Wing, for example, obviously reflects a desire to find a name suggestive of the darkness, the evil, allegedly lurking in the German heartland. Similarly, designations like *Schwarzknabe* and *Schwarzvater* amount to an admission, on the part of the namer, of the furtiveness and dubious morality of Laszlo Jamf's Infant Tyrone experiment. Yet here too irony is operative: Slothrop's identification as a "black boy," by linking him to the victims of racial prejudice, contributes to his status as a sympathetic character.

The novel's racial concerns may be further illuminated by a consideration of that most compelling and ambivalent symbol of blackness, King Kong. But before simple blackness, "the well-known ape," as Pynchon calls him in *V.* (p. 421), symbolizes repressed sexuality[6]—sexuality, that is, regarded as something "dark," dirty, and dangerous: like Kong himself, best left out of mind on a remote, savage island of the psyche. When, in *King Kong,* the white men arrive at the forbidden island, they witness something shocking— the preparations for a ritual "marriage" of a native woman to Kong.

That this is a primal scene fantasy is manifest in the furtive prurience with which they set up their motion picture camera and huddle together in the foreground or at the edge of the frame. Kong himself is overwhelmingly sexual, as one sees when he manipulates an enormous phallic tree trunk, which seems to be joined to his body at the crotch and when he later charges through the hymenal gates of the native village.

Kong's discovery and introduction into polite society can only result in massive dislocations; his rampage in New York metaphorically renders a violent abreaction. Indeed, violence and horror follow every sexual contact in the movie. An unconscious filled with scorpions takes on visual immediacy when, as if liberated by the nocturnal dalliance of Bruce Cabot and Fay Wray on shipboard, sinister black shadows swarm up the side of their vessel to lay hands on the heroine and bear her off to some vastly less coy lovemaking. Similarly, when Kong stands bound and helpless on the stage in New York, the lovers' embrace before the reporters' flashbulbs causes him to break his chains. Cabot and Wray escape to a hotel room, which Pynchon describes with an appropriate sexual image: "the room you thought was safe, could never be penetrated." But no sooner do they sit down together on the bed than the gigantic black hand comes groping through the window, with its "tendons of need, of tragic love" (p. 275). Kong's subsequent ascent of the Empire State Building, whose phallic significance Pynchon emphasizes, represents the harrowing rise to consciousness of a repressed instinctual drive.

The sexuality symbolized by Kong is complicated by its racial constituent. If "feelings about blackness [are] tied to feelings about shit," as Edwin Treacle observes, then feelings about blackness will also be tied to feelings about sex, because sexuality includes a component of anal erotism, though so strongly repressed that it tends to appear in the conscious mind only as its opposite, i.e., negative feelings about anality, often projected onto blacks. In other words, the reaction-formation by which repressed anal erotism becomes fear of and hostility toward blacks is itself an aspect of the broader mechanism by which all repressed sexual drives must be symbolized before they can surface in the mind. Thus in dreams the genitals appear as pointed or concave objects (Freud would recognize the hotel room mentioned above as a vaginal symbol), and sex itself as something ugly and frightening—like King Kong.

In the eyes of someone like Edwin Treacle, then, the linking of blacks and threatening sexuality in the popular mind merely confirms psychoanalytic theory. The association is basic to *King Kong*, whose bestial protagonist embodies all the irrational fears of "monstrous" black appetites. Consequently we are given to understand that Kong's unspeakable lusts must periodically be placated. This is merely exotic, rather than horrible, as long as Kong's brides are black women, but when he aspires to something "higher," i.e., Fay Wray, he must be lynched. Operative here is a paradox of prurience that might be called the *National Geographic* syndrome. Both that magazine and, say, a Swedish "outdoor culture" magazine show unposed nudity, but only the latter offends a racist Mrs. Grundy. The reason is just this notion that black sexuality is subhuman, hence no more offensive than the sexuality of the barnyard—so long as it remains within its sphere.

King Kong's racial and sexual overtones contribute a good deal to *Gravity's Rainbow,* and an awareness of the movie's fantasy content helps one to appreciate another of Edwin Treacle's remarks, one that suggests an explanation of those baffling and often contradictory hints about film's ability to "create reality." At PISCES Treacle witnesses and participates in the uproar occasioned by the news that black rocket troops—the offspring, seemingly, of Operation Black Wing—do in fact exist in Germany. Somehow, by free association perhaps, *King Kong* becomes involved: "Someone remembers Gavin Trefoil, face as blue as Krishna, running through the topiary trees stark naked, and Treacle chasing him with an ax, screaming 'Giant *ape!* I'll show *you* a giant ape all right!' " (p. 276). In a calmer moment Treacle wonders, "Why wouldn't they admit that their repressions *had,* in a sense that Europe in the last weary stages of its perversion of magic has lost, *had* incarnated real and living men" (pp. 276–77). The key concept here is that the "incarnating" (the word used by von Göll as well as Treacle) or "generating" (the narrator's word) is effected by our *repressions,* which normally give rise to nothing more substantial than dreams. But they also find expression in movies, which are merely public or collective dreams.

The point is hardly revolutionary. "Movies are bourgeois mythplays," Northrop Frye laconically remarks, "as half a dozen critics suddenly and almost simultaneously discovered a few years ago."[7] That film reflects the repressions, anxieties, hopes, and fears of the popular mind has become a commonplace of psychological film criticism from Siegfried Kracauer to Michael Wood (and we have probably been told a little too often that fantasies of wealth dominated the movies of the thirties, when audiences were poorest). At any rate, a director attuned to the psyche of his audience will make very compelling movies, whether he be a crowd pleaser, like Merian C. Cooper, or a crowd swayer, like Leni Riefenstahl. With Operation Black Wing, the PISCES staff attempted to be crowd frighteners, and were themselves frightened by the realization of the very fantasy they had tried to foist off on the Germans.

In many primitive societies dreams are considered prophetic, and modern psychologists would concur with this view to the extent that dreams reflect repressed anxieties that will eventually cause dislocations in waking life. In this sense movies, too, augur things to come in real life, appearing to "generate" living versions of themselves. Thus film constitutes an "interface" between a society's collective anxieties and the political and social upheavals they can cause. When dislocations do occur—for example when black ex-colonials are discovered in the European heartland assembling a phallic weapon for some unknown, frightening purpose—chances are they will be preceded by cinematic warning signals. Of course to say that movies generate the black ex-colonials and their project is a classic example of the *post hoc ergo propter hoc* fallacy (not that we shall always be able to satisfy our craving for logical, cause-and-effect explanations of such matters in this fashion). A movie like *King Kong*, or, for that matter, the movie-novel before us, is like a membrane perilously stretched between Western "repressions" like racism and colonialism and the apocalyptic disruptions immanent in them.

Perhaps because they are real, the *Schwarzkommando*, though hated, feared, and persecuted all across the Zone, fare somewhat better than the giant ape who is their cinematic avatar. They "ride the interface" (p. 731) between the eastern and western allies, generally managing to elude the hostile armies of white men on either side of them. Their Fay Wray—Katje Borgesius (so identified on p. 277)—joins them voluntarily, and their painstakingly achieved erection—the 00001 rocket, "The second in its series" (p. 274)— seems to be the triumphant assertion that Kong's phallic ascent failed to be. To rephrase Treacle, Western repressions have incarnated real and living *men*.

Kong's antitypes in *Gravity's Rainbow* include not only the *Schwarzkommando*, but the outcast and strangely sexed "black boy," Slothrop, as well. The American, however, is a less primitive and less Freudian symbol of threatening sexuality than his simian counterpart; indeed, his plight has less to do with psycho-sexuality than with socio-cybernetics. Still, with his rocket-dowsing penis, Slothrop is also a sexual monster, as both Pointsman and a young woman on his staff observe (pp. 144, 629). Both Slothrop and Kong are fetishists, too, each taking a perverted interest in Fay Wray's clothes. Slothrop appears in one of her dresses in the fantasy sequence in the "Transvestites' Toilet" (pp. 688–89), while Kong, in a scene famous despite its excision from the final copy of the movie, examines and sniffs at her lingerie in rapt fascination. Both are ruthlessly pursued by selfish men who feel mixed hatred and fear of them, yet want to use them for profit. Their enemies inflict a symbolic castration on one (shooting him down from "the tallest erection in the world"), and attempt a literal castration of the other.

Kong lives beyond his nominal defeat by a world's hostility; his myth retains its power because of its resonance in the human unconscious. But Slothrop's fate resists easy categorization. As Pavlov conditioned dogs to salivate at the sound of a bell, the unconscionable Laszlo Jamf conditioned Slothrop as an infant to have an erection in the presence of a "Mystery stimulus" (p. 84), a substance or compound later used in V-2 rockets. Apparently Slothrop was not fully deconditioned, for when the rocket blitz starts in London, the old conditioned reflex reasserts itself. Somehow it is now integral to his very identity, and when it begins at last to be fully extinguished—as the war ends and the V-2's cease to fall—Slothrop simply fades away. Yet his waning, his dispersal into the elemental mystery he has pursued, may not represent an altogether negative development. When Pynchon says that Slothrop "is being broken down . . . and scattered" (p. 738), he seems to be describing *sparagmos*, the ritual dismemberment of vegetation gods, whose parts were scattered like seeds. As the sacrifice of an Osiris or an Orpheus guaranteed the spring, Slothrop's scattering seems to fructify the Counterforce, which attempts his rescue as its first mission.

Slothrop's passing vies in mystery with the passing of Enzian, the *Schwarzkommando* leader, and with that of Gottfried, the passenger aboard the 00000 rocket. In one sense or another, each suffers the fate of a sacrificial victim. Gottfried succumbs as the hapless oblation of his demented lover, an Abraham whose knife no angel stays, while Enzian accepts the same fate at the hands of the *Schwarzkommando*. Recognizing a man named Christian as his successor (p. 728), Enzian seems less a trembling Isaac than a bravely willing Son of Man. Slothrop, too, is Christlike, becoming briefly a living Christogram: "Lying one afternoon spread-eagled . . . he becomes a cross himself, a crossroads, a living intersection where the judges have come to set up a gibbet for a common criminal who is to be hanged at noon" (p. 625).

Noon was the hour of Christ's execution, carried out in the manner reserved for common criminals. The prime archetypal scapegoat of *Gravity's Rainbow*, however, is not Christ but "that sacrificial ape" (p. 664), King Kong. Capable of taking on a variety of mythic and literary colorings, Kong functions as an all-purpose scapegoat; crucified one moment, hurled down for his pride the next. The "black scapeape" (p. 275) undergoes crucifixion on the stage in New York, where he stands with arms extended and bound—and for the corresponding scene in the remake of the movie, he even wears a vulgar little crown, so pathetic in its effect as to suggest the crown of thorns or the inscription on Christ's cross, mocking his pretensions to kingship of the Jews. The actual manner of his death, on the other hand, calls to mind the epic plummetings of Icarus, Mulciber, Capaneus, Lucifer, and other legendary personages who aspired too high or challenged the gods.

Kong's story, then, is multivalent, and in religious terms ultimately neutral. Needing a symbol that would be highly suggestive but not tendentious, Pynchon found in Kong a figure whose essentially secular passion would define and give resonance to the enigmatic fate of Slothrop, Enzian, and Gottfried. But as we have seen, *King Kong* furnishes *Gravity's Rainbow* with more than an archetypal scapegoat. Besides serving as a focus for Pynchon's treatment of racism and its unconscious psycho-sexual dimensions, the movie provides another variation on the theme of film's precedence over "real life." The film's agency in calling the *Schwarzkommando* into being retains a hint of the thaumaturgical even after Edwin Treacle's remarks have received due consideration.

Pynchon means to call into question not only the distinctions between film and life, but also the distinctions between these modes of reality (or illusion) and dreams. If movies are public dreams, as I have suggested, then dreams are the movies that switch on in the theatres of our heads when, as Sir Thomas Browne says, the five ports of knowledge are closed. The concept of dream-cinema is less fanciful than it seems, for the eyes follow the action of a dream in the same way they do a movie on a screen. Susanne Langer, in fact, maintains that film "is 'like' dream in the mode of its presentation; it creates a virtual present, an order of direct apparition. That is the mode of the dream."[8] Langer's observation helps explain why dreams are almost as important in *Gravity's Rainbow* as movies. Like movies, dreams may be thought of as no more illusory than life itself, particularly if one agrees with modern psychologists who argue that dreams are *more* real—truer to the unconscious origins of personality and even civilization—than waking life.

Dreamers in Pynchon's novel include the apparent successor to *Schwarzkommando* leadership, Christian, visited in a dream by his dead sister; Franz Pökler, who makes no distinction at all between dreams and movies; Slothrop, who does the most dreaming; and Dr. Pointsman, who has a dream that is comparable, in the professional anxiety it reflects, to Freud's famous Irma dream. Pointsman's dream follows the Freudian model in that it combines a feature of his day's activities (dog-chasing) with long-standing professional anxiety (about carrying Pavlov's work through to the final synthesis, and being recognized with the Nobel Prize). In the dream he pursues the Nobel Prize in the form of a champion Weimaraner, Reichssieger von Thanatz Alpdrücken, through a war-ravaged cityscape. Pointsman presumably knows Gerhardt von Göll, since the director films the fake *Schwarzkommando* for Operation Black Wing, of which Pointsman is one of the conceivers, but nowhere does Pointsman mention or think of von Göll's movie *Alpdrücken,* or Miklos Thanatz, the husband of its star. As if to mock the Pavlovian's creed, the dog's strange name seems to surface in his dreaming mind with no cause-and-effect justification—one of those not-so-kute-korrespondences which intimate that connections may be made in ways that are invisible and not to be accounted for by Pointsman's mechanistic model of the physical world. The fictive practice here has its precedent in Joyce, who in *Ulysses* allowed certain recondite words and phrases to appear in different characters' minds, with no logical way for the mental cross-fertilization to occur: for example, the *Nebrakada Feminimum* love charm, which Stephen Dedalus discovers browsing at a book stall, later turns up in one of Leopold Bloom's hallucinations in the "Circe" episode. Nor is the dog's name the only motif present in Pointsman's dream. Four hundred pages later we will learn that a woman named Scorpia Mossmoon breeds "Weimaraners whose racial purity she will go to extravagant lengths to protect" (p. 544). The reference to racial purity is ironic; the dog of Pointsman's dream is a champion *Nazi* Weimaraner. And finally, the "twilit canalsides strewn with debris of war" (p. 142) among which Pointsman chases the Reichssieger become recurring Waste Land motifs in the book. Slothrop, at once a Fisher King and one of

Pointsman's pursued hounds, will fish in such canals amidst Berlin's devastation, while "the dogs run barking in the back-streets" (p. 447).

Slothrop has a number of dreams, many of which involve actresses—though not in the way one might expect. In his less important dreams Slothrop reproaches his father, Broderick, for selling him to Jamf and the IG; watches Bette Davis and Margaret Dumont having an inane conversation in what appears to be a Marx Brothers movie; and takes on the identity of yet another screen personality—again, this time, an actress: " 'Oh my goo'ness,' Slothrop keeps saying, his voice exactly like Shirley Temple's, out of his control" (p. 493). Bianca, who does Shirley Temple imitations, also figures in the last dream, and since Slothrop has recently seen her alive for the last time, the dream probably portends her death in some way. Two more of Slothrop's dreams feature contact or near contact with the dead. Spending the night at Laszlo Jamf's crypt, he senses the approach of the dead scientist's "shell," an unspeakably minatory presence. Much later, a ragged and pathetic D.P. dozing in an abandoned farm house "south of Rostock," he dreams of meeting his dead friend Tantivy Mucker-Maffick, who had been sent to the front for befriending him.

Less a dream than a kind of induced psychotic episode is Slothrop's fantasy in the Abreaction Ward, which begins and ends with his drugged mind playing with the phrase "Kenosha Kid." If this refers to Orson Welles (born in Kenosha, Wisconsin), as Richard Poirier suggests,[9] it would provide distinguished directorial auspices for the cinematic atmosphere of the fantasy. As we have seen, the scatological aspect of Slothrop's pursuit of his harmonica down the toilet of the Roseland Ballroom documents Edwin Treacle's psychoanalytic explanation of "feelings about blackness." The fantasy becomes really cinematic only in its latter part. Slothrop finds himself in a kind of western, with a decadent cowboy named Crouchfield or Crutchfield, and his pathic sidekick, Whappo. In a later conversation with the Argentine Squalidozzi, Slothrop reveals himself to be thoroughly indoctrinated by the Saturday afternoon western, "dedicated to Property, if anything is" (p. 264). The western which Slothrop now "dreams" reflects Pynchon's hatred of colonialism—whether in the American West or in Africa—and of the racist outlook that is its corollary. The relationship between Crutchfield and his "little pard," a mulatto, is that of colonizer and native. Pynchon's metaphor for colonialism, in other words, is sodomy. "Crutchfield has left a string of broken-hearted little pards across this vast alkali plain" (p. 68), including blacks, Indians. Chinese, and Jews. Described as "the White Cocksman of the *terre mauvais*" (p. 69), Crutchfield is an antitype of Weissmann, who "colonizes" Enzian as his countrymen had colonized South-West Africa. Of course he also symbolizes America, whose exploitation of the red, black, and yellow races reaches its terrible climax when the "giant white cock" is unleashed over Hiroshima.

In a lighter vein, the Crutchfield-Whappo team also introduces what might be called the "zany duo" motif in the book. As much Mutt and Jeff as Shem and Shaun, the zany duo will come to include a large number of droll pairings: Trudi and Magda, Höpmann and Kreuss, Wobb and Whoaton, Fuder and Fass, Basil Rathbone and S. Z. Sakall, and Takeshi and Ichizo (these two, as Kamikazes, are involved with a Japanese-style V-2; their radarman is called Old Kenosho). At the end of the book Pynchon introduces Max and Moritz, Blicero's assistants in firing the 00000 rocket. The names, derived from Wilhelm Busch's cartoon characters, are those of the first two successfully launched A-2 rockets.[10] The zany duos anticipate and parody the Rocket deified and worshipped heretically as a Manichaean duality: "the Primal Twins (some say their names are Enzian[11] and Blicero) . . . a good Rocket to take us to the stars, an evil Rocket for the World's suicide, the two perpetually in struggle" (p. 727).

Slothrop's most important and elaborate dream—and, in its clairvoyance, the one most closely linked to the ontological and epistemological importance of movies in the novel—is the bizarre "poem, with woodcuts accompanying the text" (p. 446) that comes to him after spending a little too much time with the demented Margherita von Erdmann. The dream concerns Erdmann, and, though the dreamer knows little, as yet, about her career, it is filled with allusions to her filmography and her experiences on the *Alpdrücken* set. Slothrop will not recognize these until, later in his odyssey across the Zone, he boards the decadent yacht *Anubis* and learns more about Greta's past from Stefania Procalowska, wife to the vessel's master, and from Greta herself.

The dream concerns a woman who, like Scorpia Mossmoon, breeds dogs. When she takes her bitch to be serviced she overhears its noisy lovemaking. "The sound goes on and on for much longer than seems appropriate, and she suddenly realizes that the sound is her own voice, this interminable cry of dog-pleasure" (p. 447). Slothrop may be anticipating his later dream, in which he cannot stop speaking with Shirley Temple's voice. The woman then becomes a literal bitch in heat, and has sexual encounters with another dog, a horse, cats, minks, hyenas, and rabbits.

The dream follows standard Freudian iconography thus far. In *The Interpretation of Dreams,* Freud says that "wild beasts are as a rule employed by the dream-work to represent passionate impulses of which the dreamer is afraid, whether they are his own or those of other people."[12] The unnamed woman is Slothrop's current companion, whose company has been something of a strain on him. Whenever he leaves her, to go out "dealing, or foraging" (p. 445), she goes berserk. Her paranoid delusions—"Do you know what they were doing to me? What they were piling on my breasts?" (p. 443)— seem based on another *Alpdrücken,* John Fuseli's painting, "The Nightmare." But "whatever it is with her, he's catching it" (p. 446), and "it" seems to inspire his dream. The "passionate impulses" that he fears are both her masochism and his own sadism. However, the animal imagery—particularly the hyenas—also represents the jackal-headed men who assaulted Greta on the *Alpdrücken* set. (A reference may also be intended to a pornographic movie, ca. 1919, entitled *Hyänen der Lust,* or *Hyenas of Lust.*) The animals in the dream "fuck her inside automobiles, lost at night in the forests, out beside a waterhole in the desert" (p. 447). These details adumbrate features of Greta's past about which we presently learn. The forest is where she and Thanatz discover a wrecked automobile[13] and encounter a forbidding presence, and the desert would have figured in the movie, *Weisse Sandwüste von Neu Mexiko,* that she did with the American horse, Snake. This title, incidentally, may be translated simply as "White Sands, New Mexico"; it refers, of course, to the proving ground where one of those great lights ubiquitous in *Gravity's Rainbow* is to be tested. Her mount in the movie is the same horse that Tchitcherine rides to his annihilating, transcendental experience at the Kirghiz Light. Snake may be the "tall horse" who "compells her to kneel, passively, and kiss his hooves" (p. 447) in the dream, though she has played that scene with Slothrop recently, after a particularly brutal beating.

Part II of this tripartite oneiric poem includes a scene reminiscent of another Erdmann movie. The woman, pregnant, is being taken on a river journey by her understanding husband. One is reminded of the conclusion of *Jugend Herauf!* (the title, which puns on "*Juden heraus!,*" glances at the 1938 film *Jugend,* by Veit Harlan, infamous director of the anti-Semitic *Jud Süss*), in which Erdmann and her costar Max Schlepzig—their stuntmen-doubles, actually—are out on a river in a tub. Lest we doubt the filmic orientation of this dream, we are told that "the key color" of Part II "is violet" (p. 447)—the same color, that is, as the "violet-bleeding interfaces" (p. 484) of photographic plates and their coating emulsions. In Part III the woman is drowned, "but all forms of life fill her womb." The "key color" is now a vernal green, because the woman's saga becomes entangled with the myth of Demeter and Persephone. "Old Squalidozzi," a "Neptune figure" named after Slothrop's friend, the anarchist submariner, and given the symbolically sexual epithet, "ploughman of the deep," brings her corpse to the surface, while "from out of her body streams a flood now of different creatures, octopuses, reindeer, kangaroos" (p. 447). As her name suggests, Erdmann has become a tellurian deity, a Gaea giving birth to all creatures, which enter the Blakean River of Life. She consorts, after a fashion, with the god of the sea, as did Demeter, who brought forth a horse after being visited by Poseidon in equine form. Like Demeter, too, she searches for a daughter, and finds her in the company of a man named Death (Thanatz) on board the *Anubis*, named for the Egyptian version of Pluto, the god of the dead who abducted Persephone. Demeter's discovery of the whereabouts of her daughter gave her a special interest in the underworld, and Greta shares this as well.

Erdmann is obsessed with the idea of an existence in the black mud beneath the surface of the earth. She spends a night embracing a frozen corpse in Berlin, imagining it saying to her: "We live very far beneath the black mud" (p. 483). At the resort of Bad Karma, on the eve of the invasion of Poland, she had begun murdering Jewish children and committing their bodies to the black mud in some kind of obscure, personal, demented rite. On these occasions she dressed in black and called herself the *Shekhinah*, the feminine manifestation of the divine presence in the Kabbala. When Greta revisits Bad Karma with Slothrop, she is terrified by a peasant woman dressed in black—as if the real *Shekhinah* were waiting for her.

Shekhinah, Earth Mother, veteran of the silver screen, rape victim, madwoman—all of Greta's personae turn up in Slothrop's dream, which appears to be a marvel of clairvoyance. As a mental movie, the dream reflects certain psychological truths regarding both the dreamer and his companion, much as we have seen literal movies— characterized above as "public dreams"—doing for the audiences that patronize them. Moreover, according to the pattern that generally obtains with movies in the book, the dream precedes its subject matter—various facts about Erdmann—into Slothrop's cognizance. The fact that he must later be told the details about his companion by Stefania Procalowska and by Greta herself militates against one's assuming that, having been in Greta's company for some time, he knows everything there is to know about her before the dream. I have hitherto been able to explain how reality seemed, over and over in the book, to follow its filmic invocation. Movies, I suggested, merely expressed social and psychological "dispositions" which were on their way to incarnating versions of themselves on the conscious stage of the world; but Slothrop's dream, containing so much information about Greta's past, both on and off screen, and about her psychological problems, allows no such logical explanation. His Bianca dream and Crutchfield-Whappo fantasy appear to be similar exercises in clairvoyance. Pynchon means, in other words, to subvert our common-sense notions about causality, as he did in allowing the name "Reichssieger von Thanatz Alpdrücken" to appear, as if by magic, in Pointsman's dream. As Lance Ozier observes, one of the missions of *Gravity's Rainbow* is to call into question the very principle of cause and effect—the mainstay of Pointsman's dated science.[14] Ozier points out the contrast between Pointsman, the scientific determinist, and a statistician named Roger Mexico, a dealer in probabilities who represents the new science in which strict cause and effect is replaced by the principle of indeterminacy, which dictates probability models rather than mechanistic models of physical phenomena. Dream-movies that violate causality, then, are the fine details of the larger design that Ozier adumbrates. We begin to see film—the dream-type of film just now—becoming increasingly respectable as a mode of reality.

Yet we have only begun to consider the many ways film works in *Gravity's Rainbow*. It can be a propaganda device, as for PISCES; an analytic tool, as for the scientists at Peenemünde; a conditioning device, as for Octopus Grigori—trained to recognize Katje Borgesius as part of Pointsman's experiment with Slothrop; a source of entertainment, as for Franz Pökler or Osbie Feel, the dope connoisseur who floats into and out of British espionage and psychological warfare circles; and even a source of comfort at the moment of death, as for the gangster gunned down outside a movie theatre by federal agents: "John Dillinger, at the end, found a few seconds' strange mercy in the movie images that hadn't quite yet faded from his eyeballs" (p. 516). For the reader, film is an ontological sideshow and a repository of modern myth. It is also an important cultural frame of reference. Fewer and fewer of us have any notion of what the forties were like other than that supplied by the movies. Though Hollywood idealizes, one still gets fairly accurate information about what people wore, what kind of houses they occupied, what kinds of automobiles and airplanes they traveled in, and even what moral standards they believed in.

For some of the book's characters, film is the handmaid of revolution, as it was for the Soviets (*October* is mentioned twice). The Argentine anarchists, for example, have high hopes for the film version of *Martín Fierro*. The revolution that comes into being toward the end of *Gravity's Rainbow*—the springing up of the Counterforce—also has its debt to film, though to nothing so imposing as *October* or the Argentine epic. Katje Borgesius joins the Counterforce when she discovers the film of herself that had been used to condition Octopus Grigori. Spliced to it is a "screen test" of Osbie Feel that turns out to be a cryptic message, sounding Katje out as a prospective member of the new movement. In the film, Feel is "improvising a scenario for a movie he's written" (p. 533), entitled *Doper's Greed*—Pynchon's takeoff on underground films of the Andy Warhol variety. Feel imagines Basil Rathbone and S. Z. Sakall, the Hungarian-American character actor, engaged in a long argument about reality—the reality, that is, of a diminutive sheriff, played by one of the midgets from Tod Browning's 1932 movie *Freaks* (Feel's casting seems to come largely from his favorite movies, cited 430 pages previously). Katje correctly "interprets" the film as an argument between Osbie Feel (Rathbone) and Edward Pointsman (Sakall) about "the whole dark grandiose Scheme" (p. 535)—the experiment with poor Slothrop. She realizes that she was meant to see the film and decides to abandon Pointsman and PISCES (the Surrender no longer needs Expediting anyway). A film—nominally about knowing reality when you see it—has been instrumental in bringing one person to a recognition of the truth.

Pirate Prentice, the British spy who brings Katje out of occupied Holland, also comes to the Counterforce through a film. He sees a government newsreel that shows one Lucifer Amp, allegedly a former agent of the Special Operations Executive (Prentice's "employer"), who is now a contented beggar in Smithfield Market.[15] Someone "bishopwise" behind Prentice points out that no one has ever left the S.O.E. alive, and the spy realizes that he will never be free; even if one could get out, and if the agent in the newsreel were really demobbed, who would want to lead such a miserable existence? Nevertheless, Lucifer Amp becomes the lightbringer his first name suggests: Pirate says, in effect, *non serviam*. The beggar's last name is derived from cyclic AMP, a substance that causes the individual cells of a slime mold to aggregate into a multicellular mass. Prentice is an individual cell; the multicellular mass of which he becomes a part under the influence of Amp is the Counterforce. Once a film shows someone getting out of the S.O.E. alive, the supposedly impossible comes to pass.

One is prepared to accept what is on the screen as at least provisionally real, so long as nothing there violently contradicts one's perceptions of the physical world. But Pynchon asks that one also be prepared to see the physical world as a movie. Quoting one character's movie-language phrase about time as experienced by rocks—"We're talking frames per century" (p. 612)—the narrator imagines even geological time as a movie, the erosion of rocks "under the long and female persistence of water and air" being recorded with infinite patience: "who'll be there, once or twice per century, to trip the shutter?" (p. 613). Things faster than erosion—projectiles, for example—may also be thought of in filmic terms. A projectile's trajectory may be imagined as a series of locations. At any given moment, the projectile is in one position: its progress is a series of "frames." Similarly, at any given moment, a single frame is being projected onto a movie screen. Rock, cannonball, movie—is the motion of one less illusory than the motion of another?

The German technicians at Peenemünde[16] take advantage of this strange affinity between movies and projectiles by having aircraft drop

> iron models of the Rocket from 20,000 feet. The fall was photographed by Ascania cinetheodolite rigs on the ground. In the daily rushes you would watch the frames at around 3,000 feet, where the model broke through the speed of sound. There has been this strange connection between the German mind and the rapid flashing of successive stills to counterfeit movement, for at least two centuries—since Leibniz, in the process of inventing calculus, used the same approach to break up the trajectories of cannonballs through the air. (p. 407)

Immersed in this work, Blicero probably does not have to think long to settle on a method of assuring the loyalty of a key engineer, Franz Pökler. "And now Pökler was about to be given proof that these techniques had been extended past images on film, to human lives" (p. 407). Blicero allows the engineer to see his daughter Ilse only once a year, in brief visits that are like the frames of a film, large portions of which he is dozing through. Ironically, though fond of movies, Pökler watches them in just this fashion, dozing on and off—and confident, afterwards, "that the dramatic connections were really all there, in his dreams" (p. 579). Thus there is a kind of perverse poetic justice to his being allowed to see his daughter in "frames" so widely separated that his ability to make the connections, in his dreams or otherwise, is stretched to the breaking point, with the result that he can never be certain that he is seeing the same girl from year to year. The irony is compounded in that Ilse, the daughter, was from her conception a movie-child, as Pökler realizes when he pinpoints that conception as happening the night of his arousal by *Alpdrücken*: "*That's how it happened. A film. How else? Isn't that what they made of my child, a film?*" (p. 398).

That Pökler's daughter can, like his dreams, be indistinguishable from film is merely another example of the undermining of the distinction between film and reality that Pynchon has continually engaged in. All of his blurrings of that distinction reach their climax in the book's conclusion. The special metaphysical status of film has been so strongly established that we feel no sense of absurdity at having apocalypse presented as the falling of a rocket that has, in effect, *escaped from the movie in which it was fired*—crossed the dimensional interface, that is, and become so "real" as to be on the point of destroying us all where we sit in the theatre watching its story.

The pages leading up to the rocket's reification and the novel's apocalyptic climax present a succession of titled scenes, reminiscent of those in silent films. The titled scenes occur only in the last tenth of the book, where they subdivide the last two of the chapterlike sections demarcated by rows of little rectangles like film sprocket holes. In the movies, scenes often follow each other with little or no transition, and this structural convention, obtaining throughout *Gravity's Rainbow*, is particularly prominent in the concluding montage. The duration of scenes, however, and the order in which they are arranged, are important aspects of craftsmanship for Pynchon no less than for a film director. The American film pioneer, D. W. Griffith, for example, specialized in rhythmic, gradually accelerated cutting between two or more lines of action to heighten suspense.

Usually this involved some kind of chase, as in *Intolerance* (1916), in which shots of preparations for an execution are intercut with shots of the frantic efforts of the condemned man's family and lawyer to get to the prison with the pardon they have secured. The suspenseful chase finale became Griffith's trademark, so that his producers balked at the idea of doing a movie without a chase. As his wife recalls, "a movie without a chase was not a movie. How could a movie be made without a chase?"[17] Pynchon knows the convention and makes "Chase Music" the title of a false climax that parodies it; he imagines all the heroes of pulp fiction, radio, and comic books arriving too late to prevent the launching of the 00000 rocket: "At long last, after a distinguished career of uttering 'My God, we are too late!' always with a trace of a sneer, a pro-forma condescension— because of course he *never* arrives too late, there's always a reprieve, a mistake by one of the Yellow Adversary's hired bunglers, at worst a vital clue to be found next to the body—now, finally, Sir Denis Nayland Smith *will* arrive, my God, too late" (p. 571). As will Superman, Philip Marlowe, Submariner, Plasticman, and the Lone Ranger.

At the same time that he parodies Griffith, Pynchon pays homage to the Soviet directors who came after him and further refined his craft and artistry. The first phase of this development is summarized succinctly by film historian David Robinson: "Griffith's discovery had been to use editing to assemble individual elements into a continuous story. Kuleshov had gone farther, to show how the juxtaposition of shots can alter the intrinsic meaning of each shot."[18] But it was Sergei Eisenstein, film theorist par excellence, who worked out an aesthetics based on montage. Less interested in the juxtaposition of lines of action than in the juxtaposition of carefully chosen images or brief gestures, he aimed at achieving something subtler than mere suspense. Like the Symbolist poets, as Hugh Kenner points out in the course of comparing Eisenstein and Ezra Pound, the director fragments "the aesthetic idea into allotropic images."[19]

Eisenstein recognized that "*two film pieces of any kind, placed together, inevitably combine into a new concept, a new quality, arising out of that juxtaposition.*"[20] An event recorded in a simple, linear fashion would be utterly lifeless. "*Emotional* effect begins only with the reconstruction of the event in montage fragments, each of which will summon a certain association—the sum of which will be an all-embracing complex of emotional feeling." Yet "in regard to the *action as a whole*, each *fragment-piece* is almost *abstract*. The more differentiated they are, the more abstract they become, provoking no more than a certain association."²¹ Hugh Kenner provides the gloss to these statements: "As the cinematic treatment increases in imaginative power . . . the images take on an independent force, in a concatenation of perpetually inflected surprise."²² The "surprise" is important: Eisenstein does not want smoothness. Though the succession of images will have something of the inner logic of free association, it will still proceed as a series of shocks: "A phalanx of montage pieces, of shots, should be compared to the series of explosions of an internal combustion engine, driving forward its automobile or tractor; for, similarly, the dynamics of montage serve as impulses driving forward the total film."²³

All of these elements—the jerkiness, the surprise, the gathering power of brief, near-abstract "shots"—figure in the montage of Pynchon's finale, though the "total film" seems driven now by something far more powerful than that relic of the automotive age, the internal combustion engine. Indeed, the vibrations of a mightier power plant—"the Rocket engine, the deep cry of combustion that jars the soul" (p. 758)—become so profound that the film actually breaks. Before doing so, the film has shown us the firing of the 00000 rocket with Gottfried inside. Pynchon's narrative description has been repeatedly interrupted by the word *CATCH*—which is the film catching in the projector, prior to its sputtering and freezing and going out. The sonic intrusion recalls the one in *Finnegans Wake* where HCE's dream is periodically interrupted by the word *TIP*— the sound of a branch touching the window of the room in which he lies dreaming.

The last image to be projected on the screen before the film breaks may be Slothrop, on whom mortality no longer weights heavily: "The last image was too immediate for any eye to register. It may have been a human figure, dreaming of an early evening in each great capital luminous enough to tell him he will never die, coming outside to wish on the first star. But it was *not a star*, it was falling, a bright angel of death" (p. 760). Such false stars have been described twice before. This one recalls the rocket Slothrop sees—"Let that only be a meteor falling" (p. 553)—when he goes out to wish on the evening star after his dream of meeting his dead friend, Tantivy Mucker-Maffick. The book began at dawn with Pirate Prentice mistaking an incoming V-2 for a star:

> Far to the east, down in the pink sky, something has just sparked, very brightly. A new star, nothing less noticeable. He

leans on the parapet to watch. The brilliant point has already
become a short vertical white line. It must be somewhere out
over the North Sea . . . at least that far . . . icefields below and
a cold smear of sun. . . .
    What is it? Nothing like this ever happens. But Pirate knows
it, after all. He has seen it in a film, just in the past fortnight.
(p. 6)

Pirate's Keatsian excitement—"Then felt I like some watcher of the
skies / When a new planet swims into his ken"—gives way to horror
as he recognizes the "new star" for what it is. Looking back at this
passage from the vantage point of the book's conclusion, we find it
altogether appropriate that Pirate has, like ourselves, learned about
the rocket from film; moreover, the rocket's final-page ground zero
is foreshadowed by Pirate's nervously imagining the rocket he sees
coming down squarely on top of his skull.
    The apocalyptic rocket of the last page has at least a double
genesis. In one sense it is the 00000, fired due north over the pole to
strike Los Angeles after completing a comet's twenty-year elliptical
orbit, or passing through a time "singularity" of the type that bewil-
ders Superman (p. 752). In another sense, however, the rocket is a
modern day ICBM, the inevitable catastrophe of its use having been
determined—"predestined"—by the chain of events growing out of
the development of its prototypes at Peenemünde, Kapustin Yar,
White Sands, and Canaveral. It is fitting that we should learn to sing
William Slothrop's Calvinist hymn, for "the Light that hath brought
the Towers low" is at hand.
    Hope is to be found in the reflection that there *is* time to sing at the
end. That "last delta-t" before the rocket impacts—i.e., the interval
before the last, blinding "frame" of human history—may be a period
of any length. The end seems to approach rapidly because we are
watching a film, but time on film is a relative quantity; it can be
slowed down or, with time-lapse photography, speeded up. Even
geological time will seem to pass quickly if the shutter of the recording camera is tripped only "once or twice per century," and to record
history the shutter need not be tripped at a much higher rate. We
may in fact be a single shutter-trip away from apocalypse, yet "there
is time . . . to reach between your own cold legs," and play with a less
deadly rocket, or even "to touch the person next to you" (p. 760). In
that suggestion that we reach out to those around us, *Gravity's Rainbow* concludes on a monitory note: "Only connect," as E. M. Forster

said—and we may be able to prolong indefinitely that final shutter-trip.

If this cinematic eschatology works, it does so because of the success with which Pynchon has undermined any positivist, common-sense bias the reader may have brought to the novel. He accomplishes that end by means of an extensive program of distortion—one aspect of which is the casting of doubt on the distinctions between life and film that we have been examining. What is true of the possible interrelation between life and film is true as well of the possible interrelation between waking reality, dreams, and fantasies, or even between past, present, and future. For example, though one can discern a chronological sequence to the action of the novel, it is completely disregarded—in fact, suppressed, in the telling, and further subverted by adherence throughout to narration in the present tense, as if all were taking place in the perpetual present of the mind's private movie theatre. In addition, much of the book is given over to drug-induced fantasies, hallucinations, and abreactions, not to mention drug-influenced actions and conversations.

Reviewing all these subversions of sober perception and linear narration, one recognizes a distortion of the whole. Virtually the entire book is phantasmagorical, and one could more easily catalogue the few brief passages of sobriety than the many extended tracts of fancy. The ultimate effect of the manifold distortions of reality is to make us doubt our grasp of that reality. The book is, to borrow an esoteric label from its pages, "Gnostic" in that it calls the visible world into question. It attacks our belief in the so-called objective world's substantial superiority to something supposedly illusory like film. Pynchon delights in making us see reel become real in *Gravity's Rainbow,* and this obscuring of the distinctions between two-dimensional illusion and three-dimensional reality contributes to a discrediting of objectivism. Film gains in stature as we discover that it is not to be patronized as life's two-dimensional imitation. It becomes literally something to conjure with, for events and phenomena prove to be simulating filmic paradigms rather than the other way around. The implication is that art, however supposedly illusory, precedes life, however seemingly solid, and one recognizes in such a formulation something reminiscent of writers like Vladimir Nabokov and Rainer Maria Rilke, who simply deny the singularity of external reality, maintaining that reality is what artificers like themselves create.

In *Gravity's Rainbow,* then, Pynchon imagines a cinema more substantial, more *vital,* than life itself; consequently, to return to an illustration we have considered before, Tyrone Slothrop and Margherita von Erdmann achieve only a wan approximation of the erotic and psychological power of *Alpdrücken* when they reenact that extraordinary film on its derelict set. The set itself, with its flimsy torture rack, its wooden chains, and its tin manacles, is an emblem of real life's shabbiness beside the existential richness of the cinema. Like the shadows on the wall of Plato's cave, movies are commonly regarded as mere flickering simulacra of the world of objective reality, but the movie theatre in which we find ourselves as we read *Gravity's Rainbow* differs from Plato's cave. We will not see anything more real when we go outside.

4

"Unthinkable Order":
Music in Pynchon

Stationed at the Norfolk, Virginia, naval base in the summer of 1956, nineteen-year-old Thomas Pynchon began seeing a woman named Anne Cotton, a twenty-two-year-old Smith graduate who worked for "an intelligence agency" in Washington, D.C. Now Registrar of the Harvard Graduate School of Education, Anne Cotton remembers that the romance did not last long. She had not at first realized the extent of the gap between their ages, for he acted much older than his years, "not so much in sophistication as in intellectual interests." Nevertheless, the amorous flame burned bright for a while, with three-hour telephone calls—long distance from Norfolk—and a good deal of what he would probably describe as "rollicking." Once, she recalls:

> I had some extremely conservative relatives visiting me, and on a weekend when Tom was up from Norfolk. I had arranged to meet them at the National Gallery on Saturday morning and have lunch with them there. At that time the Gallery had bought a number of new paintings, which were on exhibit with a red label saying "recent acquisition." Tom, who was annoyed that I had to spend part of his leave with an aunt and uncle, announced that he was going to appear at the gallery, plant one of the labels on my haunch, and drag me off kicking and screaming (I persuaded him not to).[1]

Both loved music. A jazz enthusiast, Pynchon took her to various Washington nightclubs for her education. She reciprocated by introducing him to opera on her hi-fi. Whitney Bolton, Pynchon's navy buddy, dated Anne's roommate and remembers one of these listening sessions. At the time Pynchon had only two years of college behind him, while his companions were all college graduates, and in their twenties. Though interested and game, Pynchon was a bit out of his depth, hence retiring. One of the operas they listened to was Puccini's *Madama Butterfly,* excerpts from which are played at the Italian street festival attended by Benny Profane and friends in *V.* Bolton recalls a certain consternation in the company at Anne Cotton's when the female contingent realized that they were listening to an opera about the faithlessness of an American sailor—with two supposedly amorous sailors present. The difficulty was gotten around by the sailors' pointing out that, unlike themselves, Pinkerton was an officer, hence capable of any enormity. Years later, the story of Lieutenant Pinkerton and Cio Cio San would provide the narrator of *Gravity's Rainbow* with an ironic model for the brief affair between Enzian's Herero mother and her Russian sailor-lover.

They also listened to Massenet's *Manon*—Pynchon would come to prefer Puccini's version, *Manon Lescaut*—and to *Don Giovanni* (Pynchon "saw himself as a bit of a swashbuckler," according to Cotton). The famous "Catalogue Aria" from the Mozart opera was to become one of Pynchon's favorite allusions. He refers to it in both *V.* and *Gravity's Rainbow,* as well as in the short stories "Entropy" and "Mortality and Mercy in Vienna." Though Anne Cotton did not like Wagner and so did not play any of his operas for Pynchon, the author eventually came to know his music intimately and to refer to it more often, even, than to that of Mozart. Benny Profane remembers that when he lived with his parents, the Venusbergs' "fat daughter had always tried to lure [him] into the bathroom" (p. 379). Throughout *Gravity's Rainbow* Pynchon uses Wagner for comic or atmospheric touches: certain Nazi market strategists are reproached for their "*Götterdämmerung* mentality"—because they fail to give thought to postwar markets; Slothrop's Rocketman outfit is a modified Wagnerian costume looted by one of Säure's assistants; and Wagner is played on board the Toiletship *Rücksichtlos* ("Inconsiderate").

Pynchon's interest in serious music seems to have burgeoned quickly, for the musical allusion was an integral part of his writing as early as "Mortality and Mercy in Vienna," published scarcely three years after the listening sessions in Anne Cotton's apartment. The hero of "Mortality and Mercy," Cleanth Siegel, is himself something of an opera lover. At one point he is reminded of "that final trio from *Faust,* where the golden stairs come down and Margarethe ascends to heaven."[2] The single allusion hints at the Faustianism, the spiritual discontent, all around Siegel; one after another, nearly every guest at the party he has been tricked into hosting draws him aside to tell him his or her troubles. It also foreshadows the story's climax when, as in the opera, everyone meets his final reward.

In time Pynchon knew music from Palestrina to Stockhausen; moreover, he learned a good deal about the mechanics of composition, as will be seen in an examination of the serial and electronic music theory in *The Crying of Lot 49* and *Gravity's Rainbow*. While considering a wide variety of Pynchon's musical references here, I shall concentrate on the classical allusions he deploys most often and most subtly. The emphasis on classical allusions may surprise those impressed by this author's knowledge of jazz, or charmed by his parodies of rock lyrics and music hall songs. The tendency to think of Pynchon as a "hip" writer may account for the widespread impression that the contemporary popular currents of jazz and rock embellish his themes of modern fragmentation most effectively. But the really important allusions—those which examined all together reveal the most coherent and finely-wrought pattern, those which in other words reveal Pynchon's artistry most impressively—are in fact the classical ones.[3]

The musical allusions in *Gravity's Rainbow* will provide the chief focus of this chapter; however, I should like to begin with the musical allusion at its least dense, and least ambiguous, in *V.* and *The Crying of Lot 49*. In *V.* Pynchon uses musical allusion to support ironic variations on the theme of love-and-death, a theme that has often lent itself to musical expression. The allusions to Puccini's *Manon Lescaut* in chapter 3—in which the reader first encounters Victoria Wren, with the Fashoda Crisis of 1898 as backdrop—hint at a musical sophistication on the author's part that the *Rite of Spring* set piece in chapter 14 confirms. A study of these two chapters will reveal the importance of Pynchon's allusive instinct at the same time that it elucidates what F. S. Schwarzbach describes as a vision of a "culture . . . obsessed by the sexual love of death."[4]

Chapter 3 exists in another and probably earlier version: the 1961 short story, "Under the Rose." The differences between the short story and the chapter from the novel refute the previously mentioned assertion, in an early review of *V.*, that Pynchon had simply strung the book together from bits and pieces he had written over a number of years. Pynchon may indeed have used material dating back as far as his undergraduate days at Cornell, but he transformed it into a novel with utter sure-handedness, if one may judge by the adaptation (if adaptation it was) of "Under the Rose." Of course we do not really know which version Pynchon wrote first; while the short story saw print before *V.*, nothing about it suggests the work of a literary tyro.

In "Under the Rose," Pynchon tells a story of international espionage in the 1890s. The nineteenth century, as Pynchon expresses it, is "rushing headlong to its end and with it a tradition of espionage where everything was tacitly on a gentlemanly basis."[5] The story concerns two English spies, Porpentine and Goodfellow, who travel to what modern journalists would call "trouble spots" around the world, attempting to prevent acts of terrorism that might start a major war among Europe's contending imperial powers. Because of the gentlemanly tradition in espionage, the Englishmen deal politely with other spies, particularly a trio working for Germany, a country standing to gain a great deal from a war between England and France. Since the Fashoda Crisis of 1898 has all the possibilities for the blow-up, both sets of spies gravitate naturally to Egypt. As the diplomats may smooth things out between Generals Kitchener and Marchand before they shatter the frail vessel of peace, the German spies—Lepsius, Bongo-Shaftsbury, and their chief, Moldweorp[6]— are expected to attempt to provoke hostilities. If they can assassinate the English consul-general in Cairo, Lord Cromer—notoriously careless about his personal safety—the balloon, in Pynchon's phrase, will go up. Porpentine and Goodfellow decide to stalk Cromer themselves, knowing that when the attempt is made on his life, they will be least be on hand and may be able to save him. Eventually they even begin to fake assassination attempts, hoping to drive the man to cover. The Englishmen finally outwit the Germans, but Porpentine, who has violated the duello—the "gentlemanly basis" of espionage—by indulging in feelings of personal animosity towards Moldweorp, is murdered in cold blood. The story ends with a glimpse of Goodfellow, now an old man, waiting in the crowds at Sarajevo, hoping once again to stave off whatever incendiary act may be in the offing.

Except for that last, arresting detail, the story, thus summarized, sounds almost identical to chapter 3 of *V.* But "Under the Rose" is written as a self-contained short story, told by an omniscient narrator. Its action, moreover, is perfectly clear, unlike that of the same story in *V.*, which is fragmented and decidely unclear. Since the reader of *V.* approaches this story through the "impersonation and dream" of Herbert Stencil, he gets something like full information only about the figure that fascinates Stencil. And since Stencil has—notwithstanding his Henry Adams pose—a poor sense of history (as Eigenvalue, his "psychodontist," points out), he tends to be rather careless about detailing the activities of *V.*'s supporting cast. The reader—who needs to be as obsessed with making sense of the third chapter as Stencil is with finding V.—must piece together not only the motivations, rationales, and loyalties of the two sets of spies, but also their very actions. These matters must be made clear when the story's central figure is Porpentine, but when it is Victoria, whom we must always see through a glass darkly, the secondary characters and their business are perforce obscured. We first glimpse the character for whom the book is named through the eyes of seven different people, none of whom knows her, and all of whom are imagined half a century later by her son Herbert Stencil—who does not know her, either. Thus a mysterious female figure is introduced, a figure whose ambiguity is guaranteed by the indirectness with which we are constrained to view her.

"Named after her queen" (p. 67), Victoria Wren *(Reine)* is to be intimately involved with the "Things in the Back Room" (p. 410)—the ugly spiritual back room of empire itself. Consequently three of the chapter's centers of consciousness are the very natives exploited by imperialism. The other four represent a sampling of imperial European nationalities: French, German, Portuguese, and English. Only the last, the exiled and impecunious Ralph MacBurgess, alias Maxwell Rowley-Bugge, could have had any previous contact with Victoria. Under the Dodgsonian soubriquet of "Alice," she may have been the agent of his ruin back in her native Lardwick-in-the-Fen.

Rowley-Bugge does not appear in the short story, where the added focus on Victoria would have detracted from Porpentine's centrality. Victoria herself is demoted in the story to the status of mere ingenue, someone to fall in love with Porpentine's partner Goodfellow. She does, however, retain the symbolic association with Queen Victoria, because Porpentine comes to serve her as he has served his queen. But for her characterization in the novel, Pynchon adds her cruelty ("Give your cripple his shilling," she says within Rowley-Bugge's hearing); her Lolita-like past; her epithet, "balloon girl"—suggesting her early identification with war (in which the balloon goes up)—and her loss of virginity. The last, so important in *V.*, can be hedged in "Under the Rose," where Pynchon is more explicit about what Porpentine sees from the tree he climbs: "Goodfellow and the girl lay on Porpentine's bed, white and exhausted-looking by street-light: her eyes, mouth, and nipples were little dark bruises against the flesh. She cradled Goodfellow's white head in a net or weaving of fingers while he cried, streaking her breasts with tears. 'I'm sorry,' he was saying, 'the Transvaal, a wound. They told me it was not serious' " (p. 243). The irony here is that, according to Eric Partridge's *Dictionary of Slang and Unconventional English*, "goodfellow" is Covent Garden slang for "a vigorous fornicator."

Part of the irony lies in Goodfellow's determination to be a Don Juan, despite his impotence. When we first see him—in both versions of the story—he is regaling Porpentine with a description of his conquest-to-be. During their conversation, which takes place in an Alexandrian cafe, Puccini's *Manon Lescaut* comes up; apparently it is playing locally. In the story we learn that Porpentine and Goodfellow, on assignment in Milan five years previously, had heard Cremonini in the opera's première. Now Porpentine insists on singing an aria, to Goodfellow's good-natured horror. In the chapter version, however, we witness this scene through the eyes of a bored French waiter who, though shrewd enough to suspect that these two are not mere tourists, pays little attention to them until, to his well-bred disgust, Porpentine stands up to perform. The practical upshot of this method of presentation is that we know almost nothing of who these men really are, or why one should suddenly start singing:

> Pazzo son!
> Guardate, come io piango ed imploro . . .
> . . . .
> Come io chiedo pietà! (p. 65)

("I am insane! Look at me. How I weep and implore . . . How I plead for pity!") Porpentine's aria comes from the third act of the opera, at the moment when Manon is being transported for attempting to steal from the man who had kept her. The Chevalier Des Grieux, Manon's real lover and the opera's hero, begs to be transported with his beloved. The ship's captain grants his petition, and Des Grieux joins Manon in exile (she will die in his arms in the harsh wilderness of Louisiana).

The stage is set. The tale will be rather operatic in flavor: there will be love, intrigue, heroics, sacrifice. The histrionic pleading of Des Grieux, as interpreted by Porpentine, foreshadows that of Victoria Wren who, falling in love with Goodfellow according to plan, will approach Porpentine—guessing what the two men are—to ask that he "understand" and, presumably, protect her lover from harm.[7] In *V.*, Porpentine dies attempting to do so during a skirmish with the enemy spies at the Cairo Opera House, where *Manon Lescaut* is playing. Porpentine is destroyed, like Des Grieux in the opera, by misguided chivalry; misguided because he serves, in Goodfellow, a careless Lothario, and in Victoria, a woman whose morals alienate her family to the point of abandonment.

Hardly casual or adventitious, the *Manon Lescaut* allusions in *V.* satisfy our desire that every detail of the work of art reveal craftsmanly execution. Pynchon does not, in other words, decorate his fiction with the first opera title that comes to mind. He selects the one that resonates with his own theme and characterization and foreshadows subsequent developments in the novel, i.e., Porpentine's ruin and Victoria's prostitution. But we must remember that we are talking about only two brief references, one at the beginning of the chapter and one near the end (that Porpentine's death occurs during a performance of the opera may, indeed, be an unwarranted extrapolation). In "Under the Rose," however, the allusions to Puccini's opera are far more copious. *Manon Lescaut* is in fact the story's central thematic thread: the chief referent for Porpentine's character and the story's action. By examining the adjustments Pynchon makes in the interest of two different but related fictional occasions, we can discover a great deal about his artistry, while demonstrating that his propensity to allusion has nothing of the sophomoric about it.

As we have seen, the main difference between Pynchon's two fictional treatments of the Fashoda Crisis is that the reader's interest is directed primarily to Victoria Wren in the novel and to Porpentine in the story. Herein lies the reason for the reduction in the number of references to *Manon Lescaut* in the novel. They have to be reduced—just as Moldweorp, Porpentine's archrival, must be deleted altogether—to avoid a deceptive emphasis on the English spy. Only those allusions are allowed to remain that will hint at Victoria's dark future (with the prospect of life in a convent safely behind her—like Manon—Victoria is well on her way to becoming what Manon was, a courtesan and an exile) without turning her into a romantic heroine. The allusions function properly only when they help to create a romantic *hero*—when they make Porpentine into a Des Grieux who suffers for learning to love.

The hero of Puccini's opera scoffs at love, like Troilus or Leander, and of course falls in love with the beautiful Manon Lescaut the moment he sees her. Because any human feelings are dangerous for a spy, Porpentine, too, avoids love; he must function coldly, logically, and dispassionately. Human feelings and even conventional morality are luxuries he must eschew: "Certain things could not be afforded. Porpentine had realized this as a fledgling. You do not feel pity for the men you have to kill or the people you have to hurt. You do not feel any more than a vague *esprit de corps* towards the agents you are working with. Above all, you do not fall in love. Not if you want to succeed in espionage" ("Rose," p. 232). Goodfellow's amours do not endanger his mission because they are hardly serious. But when Porpentine allows himself, at Victoria's plea, to let concern for her lover interfere with his mission, he is compromised. He falters at a crucial moment and loses his life as a result.

In the story we know that Porpentine's fatal weakness—his human decency and compassion—has surfaced before, as is revealed in a flashback to one of his previous encounters with Moldweorp. Having met a contact in a Roman bordello, the Englishman looks out a window to watch Moldweorp, who is tailing him, in the street below. A streetwalker propositions Moldweorp, who goes berserk with rage and beats her with his cane. Porpentine rushes to the street and comforts the unfortunate woman. " '*Mi chiamava sozzura,*' she could say: he called me filth" (p. 236). The streetwalker's telling Porpentine how she is "called" makes them the principals in a sordid parody of *Manon Lescaut,* for Manon first tells Des Grieux how she is "called": "Manon Lescaut *mi chiamo.*" Des Grieux repeats the words rapturously in the famous aria *Donna non vidi mai,* which Porpentine also has occasion to sing in the course of the story. Because Manon moves in rather refined circles, she would never be called anything as dyslogistic as *sozzura;* nevertheless, the literal use of *chiamare* in the Pynchon story, echoing the usual idiomatic use in the opera, points up the momentary parallel between Porpentine's compassion for the streetwalker and Des Grieux' infatuation with the demimondaine.

Porpentine's is a *human* gesture, hence impure; the spy's code requires dispassionate purity of act and emotion. Moldweorp's rage at the streetwalker is not the moral outrage it appears, but rather a kind of spy's puritanism: he feels disgust at the impure, the human. Porpentine is the inferior spy for hating this "perverse idea of what is clean" (p. 236). Porpentine's compassion for the prostitute complements the reproof he gives to Bongo-Shaftsbury for frightening little Mildred Wren with the switch on his arm (the scene is retained

in the chapter version): "One doesn't frighten a child, sir" ("Rose,"
p. 239; *V.*, p. 81). Bongo-Shaftsbury's switch is the very badge of his
inhumanity: as a spy he aspires to being a perfect machine. When the
time comes to execute Porpentine (in the story) he will mockingly
throw the switch. Porpentine's human feelings will have finally
proven his downfall.

The narrator tells us that this weakness—human as it is—
paradoxically makes him at best a pasteboard hero. Porpentine
"would remain . . . an inept Cremonini singing Des Grieux, express-
ing certain passions by calculated musical convenant, would never
leave a stage where vehemences and tendresses are merely forte and
piano, where the Paris gate at Amiens foreshortens mathematically
and is illuminated by the precise glow of calcium light" ("Rose,"
p. 236). Nevertheless, Porpentine must operate in the real world, a
world much more distressingly complex than the opera world. The
operatic hero is at least not encumbered by the spy's obligation to be
devious: "Des Grieux knows, soon as he sees that young lady just off
the diligence from Arras, what will happen. He does not make false
starts or feints, this chevalier, has nothing to decode, no double
game to play. Porpentine envied him" ("Rose," p. 244).

The world of Des Grieux and that of Porpentine intersect literally
and figuratively in the Cairo Opera House, where Lord Cromer is
attending a performance of *Manon Lescaut*. Here the two sets of spies
finally clash. Porpentine's blunder at this moment—so difficult to
understand in the novel—is made plain in the story. Appropriately,
in view of Porpentine's identification with Des Grieux throughout
the story, the events in the opera house are counterpointed against
the action of *Manon Lescaut* on the stage. Porpentine and Goodfellow
are in a box next to the one occupied by Lepsius; across from them
they see Bongo-Shaftsbury with a pistol:

> "Keep down," Porpentine said. They crouched, peering be-
> tween small golden balusters. On stage Edmondo and the
> students chaffed the Romantic, horny Des Grieux. Bongo-
> Shaftsbury was checking the action of a small pistol. "Stand
> by," Goodfellow whispered. The postilion horn of the dili-
> gence was heard. The coach came rattling and creaking into
> the inn courtyard. Bongo-Shaftsbury raised his pistol. Por-
> pentine said: "Lepsius. Next door." Goodfellow withdrew.
> The diligence bounced to a halt. Porpentine centered his
> sights on Bongo-Shaftsbury, then let the muzzle drift down

and to the right until it pointed at Lord Cromer. It occurred to him that he could end everything for himself right now, never have to worry about Europe again. He had a sick moment of uncertainty . Now how serious had anyone ever been? Was aping Bongo-Shaftsbury's tactics any less real than opposing them? . . . Manon was helped down from the coach. Des Grieux gaped, was transfixed, read his destiny on her eyes. Someone was standing behind Porpentine. He glanced back, quickly in that moment of hopeless love, and saw Moldweorp there looking decayed, incredibly old, face set in a hideous though compassionate smile. Panicking, Porpentine turned and fired blindly, perhaps at Bongo-Shaftsbury, perhaps at Lord Cromer. He could not see and would never be sure which one he had intended as target. Bongo-Shaftsbury shoved the pistol inside his coat and disappeared. A fight was on out in the corridor. Porpentine pushed the old man aside and ran out in time to see Lepsius tear from Goodfellow and flee toward the stairs. ("Rose," pp. 247–48)

Porpentine's grand concern for "Europe," and his no less crippling concern for Goodfellow (apparently the sudden knowledge that Goodfellow is outnumbered in the corridor contributes to his confusion) have gotten in the way of the dispassionate efficiency that alone *can* save Europe. Ironically, Porpentine cannot help humanity as long as he feels for it: genuine personal feeling only produces a muddle of self-questioning and doubt. Des Grieux's "moment of hopeless love" becomes Porpentine's as well—only on a much larger scale. Both men have suddenly and catastrophically descended to the level of human emotions. Both are compromised, both will suffer. Des Grieux will lose Manon first to a wealthy lover, then to death. Porpentine will lose his life and, in time, Europe too.

In the story, unlike the novel, there follows a chase across Cairo and out into the desert, where the quarry will turn, and the hunter himself—Porpentine—will be taken. Des Grieux, too, plays his last scene in a desert. But before leaving the opera house, Porpentine has committed the unpardonable: in anger he tells Moldweorp to "go away and die" (p. 248). This manifestation of personal animosity toward a fellow spy, even though he is on the enemy side, is a grievous violation of the code. When Porpentine is disarmed by the German spies, he prevails on them to release Victoria (she had not been in the corridor, as in the novel, but had joined in the chase) and the harmless, unoffending Goodfellow. Then:

"You screamed at the chief," Bongo-Shaftsbury announced. "You said: go away and die."
Porpentine put his hands behind his back. Of course. Had they been waiting for this, then? For fifteen years? He'd crossed some threshold without knowing. Mongrel now, no longer pure. . . . Mongrel, he supposed, is only another way of saying human. After the final step you could not, nothing could be, clean. . . . Now Porpentine had performed his own fatal act of love or charity by screaming at the chief." ("Rose," p. 250)

At the moment before his death, Porpentine turns to look at the aged spy with whom he has so long dueled with elaborate politeness, and the narrator asks: "His Manon?" The rhetorical question tells us that the *Manon Lescaut* allusions were never aimed at Victoria Wren, but exclusively at Porpentine. The Englishman, like Des Grieux or Troilus, is the victim of his own idealism; "his Manon," the author suggests, was *always* a creature of convenience and cupidity. For Moldweorp the duello was a thing to be observed only as long as it was convenient. A Des Grieux unable to see his Manon for the mercenary creature she was, the Englishman had, like a fool, played fair all along. As announced at the beginning of the story, the "gentlemanly basis" of espionage, like the century itself, is "rushing headlong" into oblivion. And in the war that Porpentine has only postponed, idealism such as his will be one of the first casualties.

Porpentine's death and his "act of love or charity" are linked in a special way. Pynchon makes a curious reference to the English spy much later in *V.*, in chapter 14 (the paris episode). " 'The act of love and the act of death are one' " (p. 410), he says, linking Porpentine's strange "love-death" to that of Tristan and Iseult and both of these to the death of Mélanie L'Heuremaudit, the young ballerina. Pynchon's reference to "the Porpentine theme" as an example of the *Liebestod* topos may be a slip. The reference would be clear if the Porpentine episode were still in its (presumably) earlier form, but in the highly fragmented form Pynchon uses in the novel the reader probably will not have understood that Porpentine's death had been intimately associated with his own experience of love. Too much would have to hinge on the fragments overheard by the German barmaid, Hanne Echerze, the center of consciousness of section vii of chapter 3. Victoria's request that he "understand," and his exasperation at such a request, will be as cryptic to the reader as the sequence of action at the opera house and the other Stencil-blurred details in chapter 3. The true gist of "the Porpentine theme," then, is simply too elliptical for the reader to catch without reference to the Egyptian episode's other version. This opacity is hardly a major flaw, but it does suggest that chapter 3 was originally in the same form as the short story. The significance of the slip pales beside the brilliance with which Pynchon has converted "Under the Rose" into the crucial chapter whose purpose is to introduce Victoria Wren in half-light while telling only enough of the Ur-tale to demonstrate that, even before her formal apprenticeship to violence, the eighteen-year-old Victoria can be instrumental in a good man's downfall.

As for Victoria herself, she will experience only once the personal anguish of love-and-death: in the tragic affair of Mélanie L'Heuremaudit. Once again the vehicle of Pynchon's meaning will be music, for Mélanie dies at the climactic moment of one of Pynchon's most elaborate set pieces, the recreation of the historic premiere of Stravinsky's *Le Sacre du Printemps*. The riot that took place on that occasion would, in view of the affinity for such violence we have remarked in V., attract her—less moth than salamander—to its flame. As we have seen, Pynchon serves up both the Egyptian and Florentine episodes as backgrounds to or examples of "those grand conspiracies or foretastes of Armageddon which seemed to have captivated all diplomatic sensibilities in the years preceding the Great War" (p. 155). Occurring in 1913, the *Rite of Spring* riot is another "foretaste" of that war on its very eve. While there is little reference to international politics in the chapter, the oppressiveness of the midsummer weather is continually emphasized. That the prevailing sultriness can only be relieved by an extremely violent storm hints at the state of Europe itself, on the verge of a catastrophic war.

The composer Igor Stravinsky appears in this chapter as Vladimir Porcépic, which makes him the book's second "porcupine." There is little resemblance between the composer and the spy, however, though Porcépic, like Porpentine, witnesses one of V.'s affairs of the heart and is compassionate. Since his theme required that the composer be a "decadent" frequenter of black masses, a liberty the relatively pious Stravinsky might resent, Pynchon may have changed the name, along with other factual details, to avoid grounds for libel.

Pynchon also changes the ballet itself, because Stravinsky's subject matter was equally unsuited to his theme of growing Western decadence and its slide into war. Thus the title becomes *L'Enlèvement des Vierges Chinoises,* perhaps in recognition of Stravinsky's subsequent

excursion into a Chinese theme *(Le Chant du Rossignol)*. The changes
in the titles of the ballet's two sections are relatively slight. "Adoration of the Earth" becomes "Adoration of the Sun"—"a tango with
cross-rhythms" (p. 404)—while "The Sacrifice" becomes "The Sacrifice of the Virgins." In this "rite" the maternal earth is not to be
adored, but rather the masculine sun. And the sacrifice is not a
fructification, but the wanton destruction of innocence by barbarism
("Mongolians")—which is what the coming war will be. The shift
away from the positive, if primitive, theme of the original ballet,
necessitated by the role the ballet had to play in the novel, also
allowed Pynchon to introduce the inanimate automata, which would
have been singularly out of place in a nature ritual.

Other changes may have been made simply for consistency's sake.
The principals of the original Paris production undergo varying
metamorphoses in the transition to the novel. Though not an ex-
bartender like Pynchon's character, the famous impresario Serge
Diaghilev provides the model for Itague. Nijinsky, who choreo-
graphed but did not perform in the original production,[8] becomes
Satin. The designer of the costumes and scenery, finally, was a
Russian friend of Stravinsky's with the German-sounding name of
Roerich:[9] the designer of Pynchon's automata is referred to simply
as "the German." Pynchon systematically alters even the minor details: the fictional riot takes place at the end of July, rather than May,
1913, and in the Théâtre Vincent Castor, instead of the Théâtre des
Champs Elysées.

Curious as it may seem, the ballet-riot in *V.*, while indubitably
modeled on the *Rite of Spring* premiere, differs from the historic
event in almost every detail. But the real and the fictional ballets do
share a climax. That of Stravinsky's work is seen in his description of
the inspiration that led him to compose *Le Sacre:* "I saw in imagination a solemn pagan rite: sage elders, seated in a circle, watched a
young girl dance herself to death. They were sacrificing her to
propitiate the god of Spring."[10]

Stravinsky's sacrificial maiden is transformed by Pynchon into the
ravished Su Feng, danced by Mélanie L'Heuremaudit, a nymphet
whose early sexual initiation goes Victoria Wren's one better, having
been effected by her own father. Perhaps recognizing something of
her youthful self in the girl, the older woman is immediately drawn
to her. A dressmaker like Rilke's Madame Lamort, V. has flourished
in Paris, becoming wealthy enough to support the arts. Thus as the
ballet company's main angel, she in effect exercises a kind of *droit*

with its star. Since Cairo, V. has become a "peregrine," a wanderer, a toucher of the surfaces of the places she passes through—which makes her a kind of touristic Don Giovanni, for the tourist's list of cities visited, Pynchon tells us, is like the Don's list of mistresses, the *non picciol' libro* kept by Leporello. The oblique identification of V. with the legendary rake, incidentally, may suggest why her romance with young Evan Godolphin in Florence never came to anything. He had miscast himself in singing to her *Deh, vieni alla finestra*, one of Don Giovanni's songs of seduction; "the song had a negative effect" (p. 158). Properly, Victoria must be allowed the role of sexual aggressor. Even as ten-year-old "Alice," she apparently met Ralph MacBurgess half way. We learn in the Florentine chapter that it was she that seduced Goodfellow back in Cairo, not the other way around. After the stillborn flirtation with Evan she proceeds to the presumably more profitable seduction of Sidney Stencil at the British Consulate. Although V. continues aggressive in seducing Mélanie, she ceases being a Don Giovanni because she actually falls in love. She becomes instead something of a Des Grieux who loves passionately, but loses the youthful and beautiful beloved to death.

Their relationship is a curious one. They derive sexual gratification from lolling about V.'s apartment, admiring themselves and each other in its many mirrors. The scene sounds like a Cubist *tableau vivant*, and in a description perhaps inspired by Picasso's *Girl Before a Mirror*, Pynchon tells us that Mélanie is the one most excited by the apartment's decor: "Such is the self-love of the young that a social aspect enters in: an adolescent girl whose existence is so visual observes in a mirror her double; the double becomes a voyeur. Frustration at not being able to fragment herself into an audience of enough only adds to her sexual excitement. She needs, it seems, a real voyeur to complete the illusion that her reflections are, in fact, this audience. With the addition of this other—multiplied also, perhaps, by mirrors—comes consummation: for the other is also her own double" (p. 410). Here is another reason for the fragmentation of the chapter in which the adolescent Victoria Wren was introduced—as well as for the voyeuristic mode of each of the sections of that chapter. Pynchon's mirror theory of female adolescent sexuality also explains Rachel Owlglass's odd name. The "glass" in the name is a mirror, as is evident in the original German form: *Eulenspiegel.* Like V., Rachel is a fetishist, having a sexual attraction to her inanimate MG. Even her sexual relationship with the apathetic Benny Profane involves an "inanimate schmuck" (pp. 215, 384).

A more truly inanimate phallus figures in a lesbian relationship—at least in the lurid imaginings of the crowd at Café
L'Ouganda, who observe the progress of the affair between V. and
Mélanie. Satin, in particular, suggests that the lovers may use "inanimate mechanical aids" (p. 408). But in fact they do not require
such paraphernalia. V. makes of Mélanie a fetish, an object the mere
contemplation of which provides sexual excitement. Her stage
name, *La Jarretière* (the garter), seems to invite fetishistic admirers. It
is in connection with this fetishism, this love of the inanimate (i.e.,
the dead *or* the merely still), that Pynchon refers us back 300 pages
and 15 years to Porpentine. Fetishism proves a more recognizably
perverse embodiment of the archetypal love-and-death theme: "As
for V., she recognized—perhaps aware of her own progression
toward inanimateness—the fetish of Mélanie and the fetish of herself to be one. As all inanimate objects, to one victimized by them, are
alike. It was a variation on the Porpentine theme, the Tristan-and-
Iseult theme, indeed, according to some, the single melody, banal
and exasperating, of all Romanticism since the Middle Ages: 'the act
of love and the act of death are one' " (p. 410). Common sense tells us
that love and death are antithetical. Love should be associated with
life, for it is intimately bound up with procreation—*making* life. Yet
the paradoxical linking of love and death has, as Pynchon points out,
fascinated artists and their audiences for centuries. The suggestive
phrase with which Pynchon summarizes the "single melody" of
romanticism, with its repetition of the word "act," reminds us that
the "act of love" is sometimes called "the little death." In the Renaissance, men believed that sexual activity actually shortened life;
hence the association of love and death was logical. "To die" came to
mean both to expire and to ejaculate. Pynchon makes the conceit as
literally true as it was for John Donne because in Mélanie's death—a
gruesome parody of the vice the company at Café L'Ouganda impute to her—the act of love and the act of death *are* one.

Notwithstanding Pynchon's deprecation of the love-death topos
as "banal and exasperating" in the above passage, it obviously retains
its fascination for him, as the musical allusions in his early work
repeatedly demonstrate. His own metaphor for the love-death
theme is "melody," and indeed, it seems particularly common in all
kinds of musical drama, including ballets, tone poems, and operas.
Every opera mentioned in *V.*, with the exception of *Don Giovanni*, is a
study of this theme, including *Madama Butterfly, Tannhäuser, Tristan
und Isolde*—and of course *Manon Lescaut.* Our examination of Pyn-

chon's use of the last revealed his modification of the theme's traditional elements, making it embrace not merely romantic love and the death that spoils or thwarts or—sometimes—fulfills it, but the love of a good man for all of humanity—and the death such a selfless love must, in the scheme of things, entail.

With the love-death of Porpentine and his breed, the world hurtles more rapidly toward the catastrophe of the Great War, and the theme becomes increasingly distorted to keep pace, as does the music which is its vehicle. The *Rite of Spring*, considered a byword of musical distortion in 1913, seems made to order as an emblem of both violence-inspired and violence-inspiring music. The fact that the ballet celebrates the vernal quickening—vegetable "love" making life out of hibernal death—adds to the irony of Pynchon's travesty. With these sardonic variations on love-and-death, Pynchon introduces us to the war, in which every kind of love—not only Porpentine's humanitarianism and V.'s strange passion, but also love of country, love of ideals, love of man and woman, love of family—would find its courted annihilation in a ten millionfold death.

In this first novel, Pynchon refers directly or indirectly to composers representing nearly every stage of the development of music during the past four hundred years, including, in addition to composers already cited, Bach, Chopin, Tchaikovsky, Schönberg, and Varèse. He mentions even more composers in *Gravity's Rainbow*, but in *The Crying of Lot 49* he mentions only three: Bartók, Vivaldi, and Stockhausen. *The Crying of Lot 49* seems something of an anomaly in this respect, yet notwithstanding their paucity, the musical allusions here still function, still contribute to meaning, still give every evidence of being carefully selected.

Among the many things that surface momentarily in the mind of Oedipa Maas when she learns that the late Pierce Inverarity had named her "executrix" of his will is "a dry, disconsolate tune from the fourth movement of the Bartók Concerto for Orchestra" (p. 10). The tune may be an intimation of impending disorder. In "Mortality and Mercy in Vienna," Pynchon associates the Bartók composition with the liberation of the evil half of the mind. Cleanth Siegel, the main character, "knew he could listen to anything else but this mad Hungarian without getting bugged, but at the sound of an entire string section run suddenly amok, shrieking like an uprooted mandrake, trying to tear itself apart, the nimble little Machiavel inside him would start to throw things at the *mensch* who had just cast off adolescence" (p. 198). Oedipa does not pause to wonder why Bartók should appear briefly in her mind. Like the other things she thinks of, Mazatlán and a bust of Jay Gould, Bartók is apparently something she associates with Pierce. The tune she mentally hears is a fleeting presence, virtually subliminal; it is not something to which she actually pays attention. In fact, as a musical presence in her consciousness, it ranks with the muzak playing in the market where she shops later that afternoon: "Today she came through the bead-curtained entrance around bar 4 of the Fort Wayne Settecento Ensemble's variorum recording of the Vivaldi Kazoo Concerto, Boyd Beaver, soloist" (p. 10).

Needless to say, Marc Pincherle never heard of this composition, but the Pynchon reader has encountered it before. In V. Benny Profane meets "an unemployed musicologist named Petard who had dedicated his life to finding the lost Vivaldi Kazoo Concerto, first brought to his attention by one Squasimodeo, formerly a civil servant under Mussolini and now lying drunk under the piano, who had heard not only of its theft from a monastery by certain Fascist music-lovers but also about twenty bars from the slow movement, which Petard would from time to time wander round the party blowing on a plastic kazoo" (p. 419). The two references to the apocryphal concerto are not really inconsistent: in southern California on muzak played by Boyd Beaver and the Fort Wayne Settecento Ensemble, the piece is still quite "lost." Yet well hidden as it is, its existence, like so much that Oedipa Maas learns to notice, is perfectly plain to anyone who bothers to listen. It is one of those things Oedipa will begin to discover everywhere—things which were always out in the open, but not among the things the average housewife's background conditions her to perceive. The Bartók tune, the bust of Jay Gould, and Mazatlán are mentioned in the same sentence with "a sunrise over the library slope at Cornell University that nobody out on it had seen because the slope faces west" (p. 10). Perhaps Oedipa did, in her younger days, go out of her way to see things. But now she must learn to see all over again—to notice, for example, the disaffection that is as common around her as muzak.

Indeed, stealing into the ears but almost never into the conscious mind, muzak bears a strong resemblance to those left-out Americans Oedipa discovers as she unravels the legacy of Pierce Inverarity. The author adumbrates an equation between muzak and these unfortunates through the character of Wendell "Mucho" Maas, Oedipa's husband. Haunted by the endless stream of impoverished losers who patronized the used car lot where he once worked, Mucho has already had his initiation into the truth about the land of opportunity. His acute awareness of America's dispossessed is related to the curious habit he picks up on beginning to take LSD: he starts *listening* to muzak. He tries to get Oedipa to listen to it during their last meeting over pizza and beer, but she, upset about the LSD, pays no attention to him.

One of the things she might have heard is revealed in *Gravity's Rainbow,* where the linking of muzak and America's "preterite" masses is more explicit. While babbling away under the influence of sodium Pentothal in the Abreaction Ward, Tyrone Slothrop gets briefly onto Charlie "Yardbird" Parker, whose legend—"Bird lives"—Pynchon had debunked in *V.* (p. 60). Bird's music, however, does live on, and in the white man's muzak, to which it paradoxically gives the lie. Resisting oblivion, it goes "out over the airwaves, into the society gigs, someday as far as what seeps out hidden speakers in the city elevators and in all the markets, his bird's singing, to gainsay the Man's lullabies, to subvert the groggy wash of the endlessly, gutlessly overdubbed strings" (*Gravity's Rainbow,* pp. 63–64). Like the lost Vivaldi composition, Parker survives, his artistic richness and his social significance intact, in the auditory background noticeable only through an act of will. Like so much of the American blandness we take for granted or dismiss as beneath our interest, it hides some few things of substance and value.

At the opposite pole to muzak—sound one does not hear—is silence filled with music. When Oedipa arrives back at her hotel after wandering the streets of San Francisco all one night and through the following day, she is too tired to resist being dragged into a deaf-mutes' dance: "Each couple on the floor danced whatever was in the fellow's head: tango, two-step, bossa nova, slop. But how long, Oedipa thought, could it go on before collisions became a serious hindrance? There would have to be collisions. The only alternative was some unthinkable order of music, many rhythms, all keys at once, a choreography in which each couple meshes easy, predestined. Something they all heard with an extra sense atrophied in herself" (p. 131). But no one collides. Somehow, in a world from which music should be as absent as sound, these people have something of their own, an "unthinkable order," beyond what people with a normal sense of hearing have. Though usually referred to as the "hearing-impaired," they evidently suffer a less severe sensory deprivation than Oedipa. All around her, in the silence as in the muzak, is symbolic music she fails to hear. Her obtunded hearing recalls that of Meatball Mulligan, host of a wild party in Pynchon's 1960 story, "Entropy," who comes in to find four of his guests, members of an avant-garde jazz group called the Duke di Angelis Quartet, swinging energetically in total silence. Inspired by the fact that Gerry Mulligan's first quartet used no piano—meaning that the group's members had to imagine a chordal accompaniment—the Duke di Angelis Quartet have decided to imagine *everything*. But their extra senses are also atrophied, because midway through every set someone is discovered to be playing in the wrong key—or playing the wrong piece altogether.

In this idea of atrophied senses one discovers the unifying feature of all the musical allusions in *The Crying of Lot 49*, and most of the ones in *Gravity's Rainbow*. Music, in these books, seems always to hint at the extra dimensions of experience that one misses because of the narrow range of frequencies—physical or spiritual—to which one is attuned. Thus the experience of the old derelict with delirium tremens whom Oedipa also encounters in San Francisco is valuable, if harrowing, "because DT's must give access to . . . spectra beyond the known sun, music made purely of Antarctic loneliness and fright" (p. 129). The embracing of such "'spectra" is precisely the goal of the twelve-tone and electronic-music composers mentioned in these two books. In *Gravity's Rainbow* the music of Anton Webern, in particular, is invoked to suggest the extra, unexpected possibilities all around one; in *The Crying of Lot 49* the music of Karlheinz Stockhausen serves the same purpose somewhat more obliquely.

Oedipa hears the music of Stockhausen at the Scope, the only bar in the San Narciso area with "a strictly electronic music policy." The Scope's bartender has successfully grafted the language of jazz onto the new idiom: if the enthusiast has not brought along his "ax" to "jam" with, he may borrow from "a whole back room full of your audio oscillators, gunshot machines, contact mikes, everything man," if he wants "to swing with the rest of the cats." Many of Oedipa's discoveries begin at the Scope, and the world of revelation awaiting her is announced by what the bartender refers to as "your Radio Cologne sound" (p. 48).

West German Radio, broadcasting from Cologne in 1951, introduced the work of Stockhausen and his colleagues to lovers of the avant-garde in music. This radically new sound, according to music historian William W. Austin, grew out of "new possibilities for measurement and control of pitch, as well as of time and tone-color . . .

opened up by electronic technology." The electronic composers sought to transcend the well-tempered scale, believing "that the true fulfillment of the famous tendencies toward increasing chromaticism and dissonance would be neither twelve-tone technique nor organized sound, but rather a breakthrough to some new scale of pitches with more than twelve degrees in an octave."[11] The work of these composers complements Pynchon's theme, for in a sense his heroine also attempts a "breakthrough to some new scale of pitches." Oedipa Maas discovers that her country has been operating only on a well-tempered scale, one that excludes too many possibilities, particularly opportunities for variety and choice. A paranoid would find little comfort in reflecting that the American nation and the well-tempered scale date from the same century.

Music in *The Crying of Lot 49*, then, is one more feature of Oedipa's environment that whispers to her that there are more things in heaven and earth than she had dreamed of. Though few in number, the musical allusions in this novel are all associated with things outside the range of our customary perceptions; thus they prepare us for the rather more elaborate use of music in *Gravity's Rainbow*, every page of which hints at "orders behind the visible" (p. 188), including varied planes of existence and the persistence of life—of consciousness—through every metamorphosis, every Rilkean "change" of death. The book is an orchestration of "interfaces," and music—especially the twelve-tone music of Stockhausen's immediate antecedents—plays an important part in suggesting the "spectra" that we normally fail to perceive.

The chief spokesman for twelve-tone music in *Gravity's Rainbow* is the slightly daft composer, Gustav Schlabone, who carries on a nonstop argument with his "doping partner," Säure Bummer, an outspoken lover of the traditional in music. Säure's favorite composer is the lighthearted, tuneful Rossini; he despises Beethoven, whom Gustav places midway between Bach and Webern in a Leavis-like great tradition. Gustav sees Beethoven as announcing new departures, new possibilities for music, which were to culminate, given a century's incubation, in modern tone row compositions. For months Gustav

> has been carrying on a raging debate with Säure over who is better, Beethoven or Rossini. Säure is for Rossini. "I'm not so much for Beethoven qua Beethoven," Gustav argues, "but as he represents the German dialectic, the incorporation of

more and more notes into the scale, culminating with dodecaphonic democracy, where all notes get an equal hearing. Beethoven was one of the architects of musical freedom—he submitted to the demands of history, despite his deafness. While Rossini was retiring at the age of 36, womanizing and getting fat, Beethoven was living a life filled with tragedy and grandeur."

"So?" is Säure's customary answer to that one. "Which would you rather do? The point is," cutting off Gustav's usually indignant scream, "a person feels *good* listening to Rossini. All you feel like listening to Beethoven is going out and invading Poland. Ode to Joy indeed. The man didn't even have a sense of humor. I tell you," shaking his skinny old fist, "there is more of the Sublime in the snare-drum part to *La Gazza Ladra* than in the whole Ninth Symphony. With Rossini, the whole point is that lovers always get together, isolation is overcome, and like it or not that is the one great centripetal movement of the World. Through the machineries of greed, pettiness, and the abuse of power, *love occurs.* All the shit is transmuted to gold. The walls are breached, the balconies are scaled—listen!" It was a night in early May, and the final bombardment of Berlin was in progress. Säure had to shout his head off. (p. 440)

Neither is completely right or wrong. Pynchon gives both good lines because, clearly, the currents represented by Rossini and Beethoven—love and freedom—are equally valuable to the world. Interpreted anagogically, the serial music that Gustav says would one day grow out of Beethoven's innovations intimates spiritual possibilities long thought lost to modern man. Rossini, on the other hand, stands for something less abstract, more human: *love occurs,* and one sees it occurring over and over again in *Gravity's Rainbow,* against the greatest of odds and in the most bizarre of circumstances. But love is not the only "great centripetal movement of the World," as Säure alleges. There is also gravity, which, as Gustav points out presently, also has its musical expression. Both men read political significance into music, Säure hearing in Beethoven an inspiration for aggression and stupid heroics, Gustav hearing in serial music something like a paradigm of the political millennium. Säure makes his point with a practical illustration, the invasion of Poland, while Gustav speaks in ideal, almost Marxist terms ("dodecaphonic democracy," "freedom," "dialectic," "all notes get an equal hearing"). Ironically, they must both shout to make themselves heard over the "final bombardment of Berlin," carried out by the army of the world's only Marxist state.

The composers admired by Gustav did in fact make music "democratic" in that all twelve notes of the chromatic scale take on equal importance. The serial composer begins with a "row" of twelve tones; since no tone can be repeated until the other eleven have been used, "all notes get an equal hearing." With no favored tone or harmonic interval to create a distinctive tonality, however, the familiar aural orientation of music disappears. Normally one expects to hear cadences in music—resolutions of more or less dissonant elements into the consonance of the tonic. But that simple progression from "tonic to dominant, back again to tonic" (p. 443), as Gustav describes it, seemed to the serialists a straitjacket—a too-narrow conception of what could be musically pleasing.

For one as committed to musical avant-gardism as Gustav, then, the most terrible event of a terrible war may be the accidental killing, by American occupational forces, of the world's foremost serialist composer, Anton Webern. Gustav bitterly points out the parallel with Archimedes: "Do you know what kind of myth *that's* going to make in a thousand years? The young barbarians coming in to murder the Last European, standing at the far end of what'd been going on since Bach, an expansion of music's polymorphous perversity till all notes were truly equal at last. . . . Where was there to go after Webern? It was the moment of maximum musical freedom. It all had to come down. Another Götterdämmerung" (pp. 440–41). News of the death travels quickly around the Zone, and Gerhardt von Göll comments on it to Slothrop as an afterthought to a point about life and death being relative, "as to some musical ears, dissonance is really a higher form of consonance. You've heard about Anton Webern? Very sad" (p. 494). The remark about dissonance and consonance recalls the standard serialist position in the controversy over music in the twentieth century. Modern composers point out that tonal harmony has no absolute acoustical justification. "Consonance" is determined by custom, which varies from one musical era to the next. Composers ought, therefore, to be able to redefine or even abolish—as in fact the serialists do—traditional concepts of consonance and dissonance. Unlike diatonic compositions, with their modulations into more or less remote and "dissonant" keys, and their periodic, satisfying returns to the tonic, serial compositions lack "tonality" altogether and freely range a new and vastly expanded musical continuum. But many listeners, their ears accepting as harmonious a rather narrow range of intervals, find that the faculty necessary to appreciate this "atonal" music has atrophied. In insisting that our perceptions have, from habit, become unnecessarily limited, the theorists of modern music help Pynchon to document the perceptual failures he means to bring to our attention in *Gravity's Rainbow* and *The Crying of Lot 49*. The dissonance for which the serialists demand an increased tolerance, like the broader sound spectra the electronic composers insist on, can be viewed as a metaphor for the expanded perceptual horizons Pynchon advocates. More accurately, "dissonance" is for Pynchon a synecdoche representing all aspects of the neglected perceptual periphery, including the "dissidence"—the various decidedly inconsonant undergrounds—discovered by the heroine of *The Crying of Lot 49*. Conditioned to believe in and to perceive only the American "consonance," Oedipa Maas does not at first notice all the disenchanted and alienated members of the society in which she lives. But like the Vivaldi Kazoo Concerto or Charlie Parker in the muzak, they are there, disguised, waiting to be integrated into "a higher form of consonance," to borrow von Göll's phrase. As we have seen, Mucho Maas—that intent listener to muzak—is one of the unhappy few to be aware of just how teeth-grindingly discordant the American social reality is. His "whistling something complicated, twelve-tone" (p. 148), the last time Oedipa sees him suggests his instinctive craving for newer, higher syntheses.

The danger in simple American "consonance" is repression, as one learns in *Gravity's Rainbow* when the hangout of Gustav and Säure is raided by American MP's and Berlin police, who have made common cause with sinister and revealing ease. Tyrone Slothrop barely escapes by ducking out a window:

> Twenty minutes later, somewhere in the American sector, Slothrop is ambling past a cabaret where blank-faced snow-drops are lounging in front and inside, and a radio or phonograph somewhere is playing an Irving Berlin medley. Slothrop goes hunching paranoiacally along the street, here's "God Bless America," a-and "This is the Army, Mister Jones," and they are his country's versions of the Horst Wessel Song, although it is Gustav back at the Jacobistrasse who raves

(nobody gonna pull an Anton Webern on him) to a blinking American lieutenant-colonel, "A parabola! A trap! You were never immune over there from the simple-minded German symphonic arc, tonic to dominant, back again to tonic. Grandeur! Gesellschaft!"

"Teutonic?" sez the colonel. "Dominant? The war's over, fella. What kind of talk is that?" (pp. 442–43)

Both the narrator and Gustav use musical terms and imagery to impute fascist tendencies to the American liberators, but the colonel, unprepared for musical metaphor, hears only what sounds like Nazi rhetoric. Either way, the play on "dominant" and "to tonic" reveals the parallel between musical and political forms of reaction. As Europe has been tyrannized by a "master race," music has been tyrannized by a "tonic" and "dominant." Pynchon has, incidentally, associated the "German symphonic arc" with Nazi dreams of racial dominance before. The grotesque faces of Oedipa Maas's psychiatrist—"Hitler Hilarius," as she comes to call him—were originally developed for use on Jews in concentration camps, and all have "like German symphonies both a number and a nickname" (p. 18).

There is another dimension to Gustav's metaphor of the symphonic arc. Western music has been bound by its own version of gravity. Its tonic-dominant-tonic progression is as parabolic, as ultimately earthbound, as the trajectory of the V-2 rocket. Webern and the serialists, Gustav implies, would defeat this kind of gravity, because their twelve-tone system of composition abolishes tonality—both tonic and dominant. The music of the future will travel upward and outward—no more bound to arc downward than the rocket of the future that will be able to leave gravity behind forever and carry us to the stars.

The common denominator of the political and geometrical metaphors with which Gustav talks about music is freedom: freedom from tonality, freedom from gravity, freedom from oppression. But ranged against all forms of freedom are authority and power: in this context, the American liberators and the Berlin police they enlist. The Americans refuse to allow a free, "black" market to flourish, just as they refuse to devote their newly acquired rocket technology to the free, linear trajectories of space exploration, preferring the parabolic, gravity-embracing trajectories of ICBM's. Can the murder of Anton Webern, the foremost exponent of freedom in music, have been accidental? Only "if you believe in accidents" (p. 440), opines Gustav. In the quasi-fascist American future Pynchon imagines in the closing pages of *Gravity's Rainbow,* we will find that even certain musical instruments are prohibited and that objectionable chord progressions are proscribed on a "Department of Justice list" (p. 755).

Before looking at those densely patterned pages, however, and before elucidating further the controversy between Gustav and Säure, we should briefly consider the special class of musical allusions that identify Tyrone Slothrop—master of harmonica, ukelele, and bagpipes—with the legendary Greek musician, Orpheus. Slothrop becomes an Orpheus during the pastoral interlude in which he sheds his clothes, makes music, and charms wild creatures: "He's letting hair and beard grow. . . . He likes to spend whole days naked, ants crawling up his legs, butterflies lighting on his shoulders, watching the life on the mountain, getting to know shrikes and capercaillie, badgers and marmots" (p. 623). One of the legendary talents of Orpheus was the ability to charm beasts; he also charmed stones and—at Zone, in Thrace, of all places—made trees dance.

In his famous sojourn in the underworld, Orpheus charmed numerous divine personages, among them Hecate, to whom crossroads are sacred. Thus Slothrop finds himself having mystical experiences at crossroads, where he "can sit and listen in to traffic from the Other Side, hearing about the future (no serial time over there: events are all there in the same eternal moment and so certain messages don't always 'make sense' back here: they lack historical structure, they sound fanciful, or insane)" (p. 624). "Traffic from the Other Side" perfectly characterizes *Gravity's Rainbow* itself, with its nonlinear time and its scattered messages about existences beyond the present one. A kind of transmitter for some of this "traffic," Slothrop, lying spread-eagled, later becomes a crossroads himself.

Again like Orpheus, Slothrop is an instinctual musician, with "a knack for doping things out" (p. 622). A set of bagpipes, then a harmonica (a "harp") come to his orphic hand like so many charmed stones. The peasants seem to regard him as a local deity: hearing the mysterious music in the mountains, they begin to leave him offerings of food, as to "just purely sound itself" (p. 622). For the moment, then, Slothrop is the incarnation of the very thing—"sound itself"—about which Gustav and Säure have been having what amounts to a theological argument. Yet notwithstanding their differences, Gustav and Säure are both votaries of music, hence of Orpheus, its pagan patron saint. And as Orphism, the ancient religion reputedly founded by Orpheus, prohibits the killing of animals, "there is an unspoken agreement about not stomping on bugs in Säure's place" (p. 621). But there is outspoken disagreement, as usual, regarding doctrinal aspects of the musical faith. Thus while Slothrop is in the mountains, Gustav and Säure are still at it, still on different frequencies, still polarized on the question of whether or not there is anything absolute about the twelve-tone row. Gustav makes again the point he had made to the American lieutenant-colonel: " 'You're caught in tonality,' screams Gustav. 'Trapped. Tonality is a game. All of them are. You're too old. You'll never move beyond the game to the Row. The Row is enlightenment' " (p. 621). Säure, however, will not agree that the tone row represents some kind of absolute: "The row is a game too. . . . Sound is a game, if you're capable of moving that far, you adenoidal closet-visionary. That's why I listen to Spohr, Rossini, Spontini, I'm choosing my game, one full of light and kindness. You're stuck with that stratosphere stuff and rationalize its dullness away by calling it 'enlightenment.' You don't know what enlightenment is, Kerl, you're blinder than I am" (pp. 621–22).

Again, Gustav and Säure defend equally tenable positions. Sound is a game; that is, it has physical laws that are its "rules," and no compositional system, not even serialism, can be absolute as long as it is based on a physically circumscribed medium. Nevertheless, avant-garde composers show us how restricted our musical game tends to be. We have been playing musical checkers for centuries now, say Gustav and his friends—let us move on to chess. But Pynchon is not satisfied with this dialectic. He wants to suggest that there is a noumenal aspect to the world that can never be quantified and labeled with "physical laws." Returning to the question of atrophied senses, he illustrates just how much vaster the sonic "game" may be by the introduction of his synaesthetic concept of the "sound-shadow."

Modern science—our intermediary with and interpreter of the phenomenal world—tells us that the cosmos is mostly a silent void, through which sound could not travel even if it could be generated. But suppose, Pynchon says, we are the victims of an

elaborate scientific lie: that sound cannot travel through outer space. Well, but suppose it can. Suppose They don't want us to know there is a medium there, what used to be called an "aether," which can carry sound to every part of the Earth. The Soniferous Aether. For millions of years, the sun has been roaring, a giant, furnace, 93 millionmile roar, so perfectly steady that generations of men have been born into it and passed out of it again, without ever hearing it. Unless it changed, how would anybody know? (p. 695)

This solar muzak sounds like medieval cosmology updated. Men once believed that the heavenly spheres made a sublime music as they turned, a music inaudible in the sublunary world because human senses had "atrophied" at the Fall.

Pynchon's roaring sun is like Niagara Falls, whose roar is not "heard" by people living nearby. Once in a while, though, the falls freeze, and *then* the local residents suddenly discover what silence really is. In the same way, the roar of the sun is occasionally interrupted for a short time: "At night now and then, in some part of the dark hemisphere, because of eddies in the Soniferous Aether, there will come to pass a very shallow pocket of no-sound. For a few seconds, in a particular place, nearly every night somewhere in the World, sound energy from Outside is shut off. The roaring of the sun *stops*" (p. 695). Pynchon describes such a pocket in a little cafe in Kenosha, Wisconsin, at three o'clock in the morning; the lone patron, who experiences the sound-shadow, is of course the Kenosha Kid. We are invited to "sneak in under the shadow too" (p. 697), as we are invited to "come in under the shadow of this red rock" in *The Waste Land*. In Eliot's shadow we are shown fearful mortality in "a handful of dust." In Pynchon's we hear freakishly transmitted sounds from all around the world, including the chanted slogan of a Kamikaze outfit, presumably the one whose radarman is called "Old Kenosho" (p. 691).

But the most prominent among the things "heard" in the pocket of no-sound is the absence of the sun's roar—a terrifying sensory epiphany. The sound-shadow reveals the kind of sensory inadequacy first introduced in connection with Oedipa Maas, who imagined "an extra sense atrophied in herself" (p. 131) by which the deaf-mutes, living in a perpetual sound-shadow, apprehended the music to which they danced. The last time Oedipa Maas hears from Pierce Inverarity, he is using his Lamont Cranston voice. Lamont Cranston was the "alter-ego" of radio's The Shadow, created by the Kenosha Kid himself, Orson Welles—inspired, no doubt, by the experience in the cafe. When Pierce promises Oedipa and her husband "a little visit from The Shadow" (p. 11) in that last telephone call, he is alluding to his will, in executing which Oedipa will discover more than one atrophied faculty in herself. Both shadows then—the one that descends on the Kenosha Kid, and the one that descends in apostolic succession on Oedipa Maas—denote the same harrowing revelation of undreamed of sensory fallibility.

Those not visited by the sound-shadow can hear it in a piece of music—not, as one might expect, in something by Webern, Berg, or Schönberg, but in a "suppressed" chamber work by Haydn. The sound-shadow is imitated in his " 'Kazoo' Quartet in G-Flat Minor" (*Gravity's Rainbow,* p. 711), a composition that seems to have led the same covert existence as the Vivaldi Kazoo Concerto. The slow movement, as one character remarks on the occasion of a rare performance, contains " 'about a thousand ppp to fff blasts, but only the one, the notorious One, going the other way,' " and the narrator explains that "one reason for the work's suppression is this subversive use of sudden fff quieting to ppp. It's the touch of the wandering sound-shadow, the Brennschluss of the sun. They don't want you listening to too much of that stuff" (pp. 711–12).

We shall find the subversive potential of music becoming an increasingly prominent theme. One of its champions is the composer Gustav, who plays second violin in the ensemble that performs the Kazoo Quartet, "which gets its name from the *Largo, cantabile e mesto* movement, in which the Inner Voices are called to play kazoos instead of their usual instruments" (p. 711). The other "Inner Voice" is the viola, played by another of Gustav's disreputable friends, André Omnopon, whose name ("all bridge") probably indicates the quality of his playing.

One hardly needs telling that the Haydn Kazoo Quartet is a very strange piece of music. Even before the kazoos come in, the listeners begin to notice curious things, e.g., a certain prominence in the *Atempausen*—"what the Germans call 'breath-pauses' " (p. 713). Pynchon's metaphor for the way the silences begin to dominate the music is significant: "Perhaps tonight it is due to the playing of Gustav and André, but after a while the listener actually starts hearing the pauses instead of the notes—his ear gets tickled the way your eye does staring at a recco map until bomb craters flip inside out to become muffins risen from the tin, or ridges fold to valleys, sea and land flicker across quicksilver edges—so the silences dance in this quartet. A-and wait'll those *kazoos* come on!" (p. 713). Pynchon's reconnaissance-map metaphor is a perceptual one; the optical illusion becomes an aural illusion. The illusoriness, however, is debatable, because the existence of a different and actually opposite, contradictory order is being intimated. If we hesitate to concede that the hitherto unnoticed order is the more valuable one (surely silence is not finally *better* than music) we must recognize that to perceive both—or all—orders whenever possible is preferable to living in a state of semi-cognition. Maximal perception is necessary in the cause of truth, of clear seeing, for as long as an individual is partially ignorant he will be at the mercy of those with fuller knowledge. Only the Truth can deliver one from paranoia, Pynchon's metaphor for the ignorance that seems inherent in the human condition. The Truth that makes one free, however, is utterly simple, though seldom accepted because of the horror it inspires. The Truth is that our lives, our civilizations, our very planet all tend toward a final Void. We have seen what knowledge of that Void does to Hugh Godolphin, Signor Mantissa, and Oedipa Maas, whose husband wakes up screaming from his recurrent nightmare of the N.A.D.A. sign against the empty sky. As Pynchon says in *Gravity's Rainbow*, "If there is something comforting—religious, if you want—about paranoia, there is also anti-paranoia, where nothing is connected to anything, a condition none of us can bear for long" (p. 434). T. S. Eliot makes the point in much the same way: "human kind/ Cannot bear very much reality."

In an aural context, the Void may be represented by either silence or noise. Music is sweet because it orders noise and masks silence, the way Mrs. Ramsay covers the frightful cow's skull in the children's room in *To the Lighthouse*. But Mrs. Ramsay's victory over the flux was only temporary, and music will not in the end prevail over cosmic silence or, at best, random cosmic noise like the "sferics" Kurt Mondaugen listens to in *V*., which eventually tell him and Lieutenant Weissmann Wittgenstein's brutal truth, "The world is all that the case is" (*V*., p. 278).

If we turn once again to one or two of Pynchon's allusions to serial music, we will find that they, too, point toward the final truth to which one who takes the broadest and longest view inevitably comes. Describing a landscape ravaged, centuries back, by the Black Death, Pynchon invokes an eerie Webern or Berg-like song: "Behind a scrim, cold as sheets over furniture in a forbidden wing of the house, a soprano voice sings notes that never arrange themselves into a melody, that fall apart in the same way as dead proteins" (p. 621).

The same kind of music, or antimusic, as well as the same center-cannot-hold phraseology, figures in the account, in *Gravity's Rainbow*, of Lieutenant—now Major—Weissmann's last days: " 'He'd begun to talk the way the captain in *Wozzeck* sings, his voice breaking suddenly up into the higher registers of hysteria. Things were falling apart. . . . Breaking without warning into that ungodly coloratura' " (p. 465). Music like this is subversive because it forces the hearer to take views too dangerously close to perceptual freedom. He gains knowledge and ceases to be useful to those who would have him remain in ignorance, lulled by religious, patriotic, even economic lies, and willing to sacrifice what little he has—life itself—for the expediency of the state or the interests of the powerful. Webern's death seems less and less accidental. It must have been effected by the same forces that suppressed for so long the Haydn Kazoo Quartet, with its coded allusion to that perceptual revelation, the sound-shadow. "They don't want you listening to too much of that stuff."

Most subversive of all, however, is not a composer or a piece of music, but an instrument—the kazoo itself, and it is followed closely in subversiveness by the harmonica, as will be seen in an examination of the closing pages of *Gravity's Rainbow,* where both kazoo and harmonica become symbolic of a variety of things to which the Establishment is opposed. The scene in Los Angeles at the end of the book is set in the near future, in which the authorities have proscribed certain instruments—and even certain music. Steve Edelmann, the mysterious "Kabbalist spokesman" who has often been quoted in the course of the novel, has been arrested for attempting "to play a chord progression on the Department of Justice list, out in the street and in the presence of a whole movie-queue of witnesses" (p. 755). That *music* is being controlled in tomorrow's America says a great deal about the degree of suppression going on. Yet however persecuted the musicians are, their ranks seem to swell. On the Santa Monica Freeway "they come gibbering in at you from all sides, swarming in, rolling their eyes through the side windows, playing harmonicas and even *kazoos* in full disrespect for the prohibitions" (p. 756).

The witnesses before whom Steve Edelmann performed his allegedly seditious act were waiting to get into the Orpheus Theatre, which proves to be the one in which we have watched Tyrone Slothrop take on the attributes of the legendary Greek musician. The naming of this establishment, a piece of Orwellian irony, indicates that the powerful have coopted the natural leader and inspiration of all subversive, death-defying musicians. The attempt at demonstrating that Orpheus in some sense endorses (or would have endorsed) the power structure is reflected in the "title" of this scene, "Orpheus Puts Down Harp." Like the titles in the "Aeolus" chapter of *Ulysses,* this is journalese, and translates "Orpheus Theatre Management Denounces the Harmonica." The crowds scandalized by Steve Edelmann were assembled for a "Bengt Ekerot/Maria Casarès Film Festival" (p. 755), a festival whose principals are remembered chiefly for their portrayals—the one in Bergman's *The Seventh Seal,* the other in Cocteau's *Orphée*—of Death. Symbolically, then, the people were waiting to enter the underworld, for the interior walls of the theatre are "black and glossy as coal" (p. 760). Their mindless queuing-up brought out Steve Edelmann and all the other subversive musicians; with their mouth harps they tried to be true Orpheuses, dissuading people from their hideous lock-step toward death.

But the deadliness of the earlier film festival is as nothing compared to what lies in store for those of us now inside the theatre watching the apocalyptic finale of the movie *Gravity's Rainbow.* At the sounding of the nuclear-attack warning siren, the scene shifts from Los Angeles back to the actual launch of the 00000 rocket, the instrument of death for all of us who patronize the Orpheus. Inside the rocket, by means of a one-way radio link, Major Weissmann's catamite Gottfried hears his own launching described to him by his demented lover: " 'The edge of evening . . . the long curve of people all wishing on the first star. . . . Always remember those men and women along the thousands of miles of land and sea. The true moment of shadow is the moment in which you see the point of light in the sky. The single point, and the Shadow that has just gathered you in its sweep" (pp. 759–60). The Orpheus Theatre queue hyperbolically lengthens to a world-girdling "curve of people." The shadow here is literally that of night, which advances across the path of the launched-at-twilight rocket. But when Weissmann's second use of the word *shadow* is capitalized, it has become an emblem of the mystery into which Gottfried voyages. He travels, after *Brennschluss,* faster than the speed of sound—which is to say, in a version of the sound-shadow (itself "the *Brennschluss* of the sun"). And since the rocket strikes before it can be heard, its victims die in the same pocket of no-sound.

While the Shadow takes on all the resonance we earlier discovered in the shadow-trope, it refers chiefly now to death: as in Psalm 23 ("the valley of the shadow of death") or Eliot's "The Hollow Men," where, repeated knell-like, the word tolls us into "death's twilight kingdom." Eliot's poem seems almost to dictate Pynchon's final imagery:

> Between the idea
> And the reality
> . . . .
> Falls the Shadow

The Shadow intervenes between the "idea" of the rocket that we watch on the movie screen and the "reality" of the rocket that descends on the theatre. As the rocket materializes, it acquires "essence," like any other real thing:

> Between the essence
> And the descent
> Falls the Shadow

Yet Gottfried voyages into space as well as death, and Pynchon intimates that the one is as full of mystery and promise as the other. The possibility, in space, of discoveries among distant worlds is as spiritually quickening as the possibility, in death, of a survival of the individual consciousness, or "soul," after the dead proteins unlock. Gottfried does not simply die or disappear; he is *transformed*. His fate dramatizes the mystical ontology set forth by Wernher von Braun—one of the creators of Gottfried's rocket—in the epigraph to Pynchon's first chapter, "Beyond the Zero": "Nature does not know extinction; all it knows is transformation. Everything science has taught me, and continues to teach me, strengthens my belief in the continuity of our spiritual existence after death" (p. 1). In death as in space Gottfried will experience those "spectra beyond the known sun" which we have found to constitute the numenal aura accompanying many of Pynchon's musical allusions. Coupled with excursions into the fantastic and the surreal (dancing deaf-mutes, sound-shadows, modern Orphism, the Other Side, et cetera), the musical allusions hint at orders of being far beyond the sober faculties of rational-minded twentieth-century man. But modern man desperately needs to be "transected" into these realms, for his peculiar affliction, as Pynchon reminds us in *The Crying of Lot 49,* is the "exitlessness, the absence of surprise to life" (p. 170). Pynchon's musical allusions tell us, finally, that we must discover and exercise whatever sense or senses have atrophied, in hopes that one day we may hear an "unthinkable order of music," played by some astral Orpheus to lead us back into the sunlight, out of "our crippl'd Zone."

5

Intersecting Worlds: Language and Literature in Pynchon

In 1960, apparently to support himself while writing *V.*, Pynchon took a job with the Boeing Company in Seattle. According to Mathew Winston, "He worked for Boeing from February 2, 1960, to September 13, 1962, not as editor of a house organ, as has been commonly reported, but as an 'engineering aide' who collaborated with others on writing technical documents."[1] But Walter Bailey, one of Pynchon's coworkers ("a couple of desks over") in Boeing's giant Developmental Center, remembers that he wrote for an intramural sheet called the "Minuteman Field Service News" (to be distinguished from the company's official house organ, *The Boeing News*).[2] Pynchon and Bailey worked in the Minuteman Logistics Support Program; Bailey notes that the author had a "Secret" clearance, so the FBI must have a pretty good file on him.

The jolly tar we glimpsed in the last chapter, wont to set the barracks on a roar with his dirty limericks, or to plot kidnapping at the National Gallery, was now a Navy veteran and college graduate—and rather introverted. Bailey remembers him as a taciturn and withdrawn young man whose apparent misanthropy did not make him particularly well-liked. Occasionally, to isolate himself further from the people and noise around him, he would shroud himself in the enormous stiff sheets of paper used for engineering drawings and work within this cocoon, like an aerospace Bartleby, by whatever light filtered in. But his physical appearance, at least, had changed for the better. The man whom both Anne Cotton and Whitney Bolton described as "*very* skinny" was now attractive and virile-looking, with a great shock of black hair and a black moustache. Bailey also describes the Pynchon of this time as "stocky," but perhaps the fifteen-year-old stream of memory eddies here.

Bailey makes an interesting point concerning Pynchon's orientation with regard to the two cultures. Sitting among all those engineers, scientists, and rocketeers, the scientific Pynchon was apparently little stimulated—at least to conversation and friendships. While Bailey does not claim to have known Pynchon well, he was one of the few people to whom the author ever spoke. An avid reader and former employee of the Macmillan Company publishing house, Bailey made a casual literary reference one day, which generated an immediate and enthusiastic response from Pynchon. The young author was not looking for contacts in the publishing world, for Lippincott had already taken an option on *V.* He was simply starved for literary conversation. Bailey came away with the impression that Pynchon was formidably well read, "very literate." Asked if he means that Pynchon was out of his depth in an engineer's world, Bailey said that, no, he was quite competent to write about technical matters,[3] but that there was no question about the area of his main interest and enthusiasm.

Bailey's testimony will not surprise anyone who considers the Joycean multiplicity of Pynchon's literary allusions, which range not only English and American literature, but the literatures of twelve or so other countries as well, among them Argentina (Borges, Lugones, Hernandez), France (Baudelaire, Rimbaud, de Sade), Italy (Dante, Machiavelli, Manzoni, D'Annunzio), and Germany (Rilke, Goethe, Heine, the Brothers Grimm). Less liberally represented, the literatures of Greece, Ireland, Canada, Russia, Kazakhstan, Namibia, and the Levant figure in Pynchon's references to Homer, Joyce, John McCrae, Nabokov, folk ballads and tales, and the Bible, respectively. In English he turns most often to his fellow writers of fiction, citing Dickens, Conrad, Santayana, Bunyan, Kipling, Hemingway, Thurber, Bram Stoker, Victor Appleton, Henry Miller, Compton Mackenzie, Charles Dodgson, Ishmael Reed, Djuna Barnes, and Philip Roth. Poets whose work he touches on include Pound, Keats, Coleridge, Milton, Tennyson, Poe, Randall Jarrell, Emily Dickinson, and T. S. Eliot. He also refers to prose writers such as Walter Pater, Sir Thomas Browne, Thomas Hooker (the American theologian), and Henry Adams. Pynchon seems at first glance to slight playwrights, alluding only to Shakespeare in addition to the dramatists already mentioned. But as I shall show, there are submerged allusions to a host of Jacobean and Caroline playwrights in *The Courier's*

Tragedy, that wonderful parody of revenge drama in *The Crying of Lot 49.*

The subject of Pynchon's literary debts is one that has already received a good deal of critical attention. Joseph Slade has turned more earth in this critical garden than anyone else. Analyzing the literary debts to Conrad, Machiavelli, Adams, and Eliot, particularly, he concentrates on the influence of these writers on the young Pynchon, the author of *V.* and the short stories. Other critics have discussed the influence of Jorge Luis Borges, Henry Adams, Robert Graves, Nathanael West, and Vladimir Nabokov (one of Pynchon's teachers at Cornell). A discussion of Pynchon's literary allusions at anything less than book-length must necessarily be selective, but in the following an attempt will be made to consider not only such central literary presences in Pynchon's fiction as Rilke and various medieval and modern practitioners of the quest-romance, but also less obvious ones like Charles Dodgson and E. M. Forster.

In the preceding chapters it has been impossible to avoid excursions into the subject matter of the present one. Literary matters already considered include Pater's and Machiavelli's influence on the Florentine episode of *V.,* Keats's presence in the opening and close of *Gravity's Rainbow,* Coleridge's contribution to the character of Hugh Godolphin, and Eliot's, Joyce's, and perhaps Forster's more general sway in all of Pynchon's writings. Much remains to be said, however, not only about Pynchon's uses of his reading, but also about his attitude toward literature's essential stylistic and linguistic elements—as revealed, for example, in the subtlety and mystery discovered by Oedipa Maas in language itself. With a sinister connectedness exfoliating all around her, this budding paranoid finds in metaphor and paronomasia yet more—and vaster—connectedness, for figures of speech like these establish identity between supposedly disparate things, demonstrating new and appalling possibilities for phenomenal fluidity to a mind craving stability, certainty, and rest. Oedipa seeks the Word that will order all words and all things, but while the words and things mockingly show forth their intricate and increasingly remote concatenation, the key to their connectedness continually eludes her.

Many of Pynchon's literary allusions function like his musical allusions, contributing to a mythology of the Other Side. Some do so by invoking the resonance and authority of earlier literary excursions into the fantastic; others, like the echoes of Eliot's "The Hollow Men," do so simply because they concern death, presumably the transition to whatever Other Side exists. Early in *Gravity's Rainbow*, Pynchon quotes Emily Dickinson's "Because I Could Not Stop for Death," the opening lines of which Tyrone Slothrop's grandfather took for an epitaph. With its centuries-dead speaker, the poem predicates an immortality of indeterminate theology, and so contributes something to Pynchon's imagined supraentropic order. *Gravity's Rainbow* may also contain some oblique references to another voice-from-the-dead poem, Randall Jarrell's "Death of the Ball-Turret Gunner." Built on paradox—death occurs at birth, the moment of awakening from an intrauterine "dream of life"— Jarrell's poem complements Pynchon's own paradoxical reflections on life and death (and war and peace) as "states" capable of intermingling. But chief among the literary meditations on death and its aftermath cited or echoed in the novel are the many quotations from the German poet Rilke, whose obsession with mortality often found expression in a poignant mixture of fatalism and affirmation. That *Gravity's Rainbow* can easily assimilate Rilke's "Angels," those transcendent beings that bear witness to orders of experience and value remote from ordinary human awareness, is no mean testimony to its scale and to the confidence and daring of its author.

To do justice to the Rilke allusions and their contexts, we shall need to touch on Pynchon's use of Jungian psychology. Because it subsumes much of the Eastern and primitive thought, and much of the mandalic, alchemical, and Kabbalistic lore that Pynchon exploits, Jung's system provides one thread to guide the reader through the labyrinth. Of course Pynchon probably adheres to Jung no more than to Freud. Their systems serve him simply as more or less cogent fictions, and he makes use now of one, now the other. Nonetheless, he may find Jung's theories more congenial to his own grand fictions. The great feminine archetype developed in *V.* and the transcendental orders adumbrated in *Gravity's Rainbow* fit much more readily into the Jungian world picture than into the Freudian; moreover, Jung may be said to have—he is in fact sometimes criticized for having—enriched art and literature as much as he advanced the science of psychology, and Pynchon would respond positively to such breadth and eclecticism.

An embracer of fictions, Pynchon does not slight religious mythology, developing archetypes, themes, and topoi from a variety of faiths. Christianity alone contributes grails, scapegoats, Holy Cities, Pentecosts, and Eucharists to his novels. Though he often waxes ironic about these things, he never becomes cynical, and one suspects that Oedipa Maas's poignant thirst for revelation is in reality a projection of Pynchon's own. His devotion to the quest plot, a consideration of which will conclude this chapter, furnishes the grounds for such an inference. Literary quests, with the exception of detective stories, tend naturally to reflect the great and traditional questions about the human condition; whatever the religious certainties of the cultures that produce quest literature, it tends to express man's existential anxiety. Pynchon's devotion to the quest plot exemplifies as nothing else his desire to repudiate, undermine, or transcend the modern Waste Land, too long accepted fatalistically as entropy's proving ground. Thus in *Gravity's Rainbow* his fictive experimentation with fantasy, magic, and the occult—all sanctioned by the quest literature which he imitates and to which he alludes—amounts to a calculated assault on the world view dictated by the concept of entropy. Like so many modern literary careers, Pynchon's has itself been a quest, a quest for fictional modes of confrontation with modern man's sense of the absurdity of his existence. Consequently, he seems to imply that the quest, however contrived, has a value irrespective of the sought-after grail's authenticity or spuriousness. Yet he also insists on the possibility of finding or generating some grail less factitious than the ones pursued by Herbert Stencil, Oedipa Maas, and Tyrone Slothrop. Such a grail, existing only in imagination or fiction today, but perhaps ratified by science tomorrow, would again define, again provide a direction for, the aspirations of the human intellect and the loyalties of the human heart.

As I have pointed out before, many of Pynchon's literary allusions—a phrase or *mise en scène* from T. S. Eliot, an echo of Sir Thomas Browne—seem to hide like exotic birds in the rich foliage of his prose. Walter Pater's effacement as contributor to the description of Botticelli's *Birth of Venus* in the Florentine chapter of *V.* provides a typical example of this allusive diffidence. As prolegomenon to an analysis of the numerous but highly oblique allusions in *The Courier's Tragedy*, the Jacobean revenge drama seen by Oedipa Maas in *The Crying of Lot 49*, I should like briefly to consider another example, one brought to my attention by Andrew Welsh. Given Pynchon's fascination with the South Pole and accounts of it, one might expect to find traces in his fiction of Edgar Allan Poe's novella of Antarctic adventure, *The Narrative of Arthur Gordon Pym of Nantucket*. Poe's tale describes an imaginary voyage of exploration which culminates in the arrival of the eponymous hero at a great chasm—

presumably the South Pole. According to Edward Davidson, Poe was influenced by a theory propounded by John Cleves Symmes (better known as a jurist than as a theoretical geographer) that there were "holes at the poles"—leading to vast hollow regions peopled by an ancient race.[4] One thinks again of the Florentine chapter of *V.*, in which Sidney Stencil allegedly comes to the conclusion, based on what he has been able to learn about Hugh Godolphin and his polar experiences, that "a barbaric and unknown race . . . are even now blasting the Antarctic ice with dynamite, preparing to enter a subterranean network of natural tunnels" (p. 197).

Gravity's Rainbow also contains indirect references to *Pym*. The narrator's hatred of whiteness in Pynchon's novel reminds one of the violent feelings toward the color white evinced by the black savages—even their teeth are black—who populate Poe's Antarctic. So vehemently do they abhor whiteness that they murder the band of sailors with whom Pym travels. The enigma of their strange antipathy deepens at the end of the tale, for the protagonist, escaping from them, is carried by a swift current inexorably south, through a shower of white flakes which are neither ash nor snow. Everything is silent and white. Like Gottfried in the 00000 rocket, Pym voyages into mystery. The "Other Kingdom" to which Gottfried tends, as we shall see, at his death and at every coupling with Blicero, sounds unmistakably polar: "He approached the gates of that Other Kingdom, felt the white gigantic muzzles somewhere inside, expressionless beasts frozen white" (p. 722). Pym's story, which Poe pretends he has been constrained to publish in fragmentary form, breaks off as his small boat approaches the pole. Like "the last image" on the *Gravity's Rainbow* movie screen, which "may have been a human figure" (p. 760), the last image in *Pym* is an enigmatic human shape: "And now we rushed into the embraces of the cataract, where a chasm threw itself open to receive us. But there arose in our pathway a shrouded human figure, very far larger in its proportions than any dweller among men. And the hue of the skin of the figure was of the perfect whiteness of the snow."[5]

Pynchon's skirting of explicit reference to Poe's novella demonstrates the subtlety of his allusive instinct and suggests the probing called for by a *tour de force* like *The Courier's Tragedy*, where the density of allusion is very high. This play, in Pynchon's synopsis, is so perfect that one tends to take it for granted. We know without being told that it is brilliant parody, but unless we pause to analyze it, we remain in ignorance of the variety of its elements, and of the learning manifested in that variety. Some critics think that Pynchon "works up" areas of knowledge to use in his fiction. *The Courier's Tragedy* probably represents both working up and an iceberg's tip of long-standing literary erudition. Not only does Pynchon know intimately the genre he parodies, he knows as well its scholarly problems, vocabulary, and methodology.

A summary of *The Courier's Tragedy* will help to show Pynchon's specific dramaturgic borrowings. *Hamlet,* the most famous of all revenge tragedies, provides the dramatic problem. Like the prince of Denmark, the courier Niccolò is the son of a dear father murdered; the duchy of Faggio, like the kingdom of Denmark, has been usurped. Niccolò, the rightful heir to the duchy, may not survive the machinations of the regent, his own illegitimate half-brother, Pasquale, who is abetted by the scheming Duke Angelo of neighboring Squamuglia. It was Angelo who poisoned the father of Niccolò and Pasquale, but Faggio's regent, the fruit of an illicit union between the late duke and Francesca, sister and sometime mistress of the Duke of Squamuglia, does not seem to mind his father's taking-off by his jealous uncle. A veritable Cesare Borgia, Duke Angelo now plans to unite the neighboring duchies by marrying Francesca to her own son. But the intended marriage does not go smoothly; a corrupt cardinal proves to be not corrupt enough to sanction a mother-son duo at the altar, and has to be martyred gruesomely.

Meanwhile Niccolò, a model of filial piety, lurks at the Squamuglian court disguised as a Thurn and Taxis mail courier, awaiting an opportunity to avenge his father's murder. His life is continually in danger, since both Angelo and Pasquale are trying to find him out and have him killed. A faithful retainer of the Faggian ducal household, one Ercole, saves Niccolò from death at least twice. Eventually, however, Ercole is captured, tried by kangaroo court, and summarily executed—but not before he has managed to send word of the projected mother-son marriage back to Faggio. An outraged mob of Faggians then murders Pasquale, whereupon "a complete nonentity" named Gennaro becomes interim head of state until Niccolò can be called home. At just this moment Angelo, still unaware of the courier's true identity, has dispatched him with a letter designed to placate the Faggians; but after his departure Angelo finds out who he really is and arranges for agents of Trystero, the deadly enemies of Thurn and Taxis, to know about his mission. As expected, the Trystero agents waylay and murder the hapless courier. His "tragedy" is that he wears the Thurn and Taxis colors only as a disguise, a "vizard," as Pynchon calls it in his best seventeenth-century diction. After his death, the letter he was carrying is found to have been miraculously transformed into a full confession by Angelo. Inspired by the miracle, Gennaro and the Faggians invade Squamuglia and lay it waste, killing its villainous duke in the process.

The plot is palpably absurd, yet not recognizably different from plots typical of the dramatic subgenre being spoofed, for Pynchon has in fact cannibalized all the most famous revenge plays to make *The Courier's Tragedy* more convincing as their epitome. One traces what Pynchon would call the "etiology" of the play in the villainies of the ducal courts—the poisonings, dismemberment, torture, incest, fornication, and general "Machiavellian" viciousness that are all standard revenge tragedy fare. The action of *The Courier's Tragedy*, however disgusting or improbable, almost always has precedents in the works of Webster, Tourneur, Kyd, Ford, and Shakespeare. When Duke Angelo chortles over the ink he uses because it is made from the fished-up bones of Faggio's Lost Guard, all fifty of whom he had had murdered years ago, and thrown in the lake—*"This pitchy brew in France is 'encre' hight; / In this might dire Squamuglia ape the Gaul, / For 'anchor' it has ris'n, from deeps untold"* (p. 70)—one is reminded of the ink imagery in Cyril Tourneur's *The Revenger's Tragedy:* "His violent act has . . . / Thrown ink upon the forehead of our state / Which envious spirits will dip their pens into / After our death, and blot us in our tombs" (I.ii.2–6). And there are numerous other parallels. The tearing out of an informer's tongue by Ercole recalls similar acts in Kyd's *Spanish Tragedy* and Shakespeare's *Titus Andronicus.* The impaling of the tongue on Ercole's rapier resembles the impaling of Annabella's heart at the end of *'Tis Pity She's a Whore,* a play which also turns on the issue of incest. A brother's opposition to his sister's desires also figures in Webster's *The Duchess of Malfi,* which contains another fleshly and degenerate cardinal, as does *The White Devil.* Ercole's mock trial may have been inspired by the famous one in *The White Devil,* though there are trials in other Webster plays, and in those of Philip Massinger. As we have already seen, the necessity of avenging a poisoned father, and regaining a usurped state, comes from *Hamlet.* Niccolò's letter, which "miraculously" (but perhaps with the help of his Trystero murderers) turns into a complete confession by Angelo, recalls the almost as miraculously changed letter with which, in *Hamlet,* Rosencrantz and Guildenstern arrive in England. Again an instrument of treachery is transformed into an instrument of justice.

The parody of revenge tragedy extends also to its technical aspects, for both the structure and the language of *The Courier's Tragedy* have the air of authenticity. Pynchon carefully sketches in all five acts and approximately fourteen individual scenes; he also "quotes" a total of thirty-six lines, faithfully rendering not only meter and cadence, but also archaisms ("vizard," "hight"), periphrasis ("pitchy brew" for ink), elision ("ris'n"), Latinisms ("tegument"), and bilingual puns (*encre-encore*-anchor). Sustained metaphor and classical allusion appear too, as when Pasquale recalls his plan to entice the enfant Niccolò into a cannon whose powder he would then ignite to create a noisy polyphony of saltpetre and sulfur, as the child was blown *"Out in a bloody rain to feed our fields / Amid the Maenad roar of nitre's song / And sulfur's cantus firmus"* (p. 66). Niccolò would thus have become another Orpheus, as it was frenzied Maenads who dismembered and scattered the legendary musician. In his zeal for dramaturgical authenticity, Pynchon even quotes rhymed couplets for the conclusions of two of the acts. Curiously, each of these acts ends with two rhymed couplets instead of the usual one. This detail suggests that Pynchon used John Ford's *'Tis Pity She's a Whore*—two acts of which also end with the rare double couplets— as one model for *The Courier's Tragedy*.

The imaginary author of this play has as many models as the play itself, and a consideration of the real playwrights behind Richard Wharfinger will demonstrate Pynchon's attention to the minutiae of plausibility. The man whom Oedipa Maas refers to as "the historical Wharfinger" (p. 151) probably owes something to each of the three legitimate playwrights anthologized with him in Emory Bortz's *Plays of Ford, Webster, Tourneur, and Wharfinger,* a copy of which Oedipa goes to so much trouble to buy. When Oedipa visits Bortz the first time, he shows her a travel book of Charles I's time, written by the tiresomely pious Karl Baedeker of that age, Diocletian Blobb, (himself a composite of Thomas Coryat, Peter Mundy, and Fynes Moryson). " 'Lucky for me,' said Bortz, 'Wharfinger, like Milton, kept a commonplace book, where he jotted down quotes and things from his reading. That's how we know about Blobb's *Peregrinations*' " (p. 157). The commonplace book makes Wharfinger sound like Webster, who worked from one to the extent that he became notorious for his borrowings. Webster's commonplace book, however, has had to be reconstructed from evidence of borrowing in the plays themselves. But one of his sources, according to R. W. Dent,[6] may have been Coryat's *Crudities,* a travel book answering the description of

Blobb's *Peregrinations*. If Wharfinger read Blobb before he wrote *The Courier's Tragedy*, he is, strictly speaking, more of a "Caroline" dramatist than a "Jacobean" one. This dating tends to align him with Ford, or perhaps Philip Massinger, the pronunciation of whose name is closest to that of Pynchon's playwright. We can infer the pronunciation of the name because it appears as a common noun in *Webster's New Collegiate Dictionary*, which tells us that a wharfinger manages a commercial wharf. Though the word is properly pronounced [wárf-in-jer], one tends to think of it as "wharf-finger"— i.e., a jetty or pier-style wharf pointing like a finger into the deep, a direction eventually followed by Randolph Driblette, who directed the production of *The Courier's Tragedy* that Oedipa sees. He had himself taken the part of Gennaro, and he wears the costume when he commits suicide.

Pynchon's knowledge also embraces the seventeenth-century ambience, the social and religious currents which found their expression—or their object lesson—in a theatre of violence and amoral intrigue. So brutal is the world of revenge tragedy that a number of critics incline toward the view of Driblette, who tells Oedipa that *The Courier's Tragedy* "was written to entertain people. Like horror movies" (p. 77). Hardin Craig, speaking of *The Revenger's Tragedy*, could be describing revenge drama generally when he writes: "The whole play is set in a world so wicked as to be beyond belief."[7] Pynchon describes this incredibly wicked world, along with the people who found it entertaining, in a passage of great rhetorical dexterity; in the following, the reader must wait until the last word to discover whether all the adjectives modify "audiences" or "landscape": "Oedipa found herself . . . sucked utterly into the landscape of evil Richard Wharfinger had fashioned for his 17th-century audiences, so preapocalyptic, death-wishful, sensually fatigued, unprepared, a little poignantly, for that abyss of civil war that had been waiting, cold and deep, only a few years ahead of them" (p. 65). The passivity and vitiation of the audiences find their complement in the violent emotion on the stage. Gāmini Salgādo, another Tourneur critic, looks to this violence under the proscenium—and finds prefigured the same abyss: "*The Revenger's Tragedy* has a frenetic, panic-stricken kind of rhythm, the pulse beat of a world rushing headlong to its final and inevitable annihilation."[8]

Pynchon renders the atmosphere and nuances of Jacobean dramaturgy with great care, relying not merely on the standard flamboyant villainies, but also on characterizations as subtle as that

of Ercole, for whom "faithful retainer"—the epithet previously used
to describe him—is perhaps too charitable an appelation. "Faithful"
accurately characterizes few of the people in these plays, and Pynchon makes the point that Ercole, "secretly involved with dissident
elements in the court of Faggio who want to keep Niccolò alive" (p.
66), has, like everyone else, a special interest, a complex motive.
Understandably, "Jacobean" is for Pynchon a synonym for "decadent"; thus when he mentions, in *V.*, that the painter Slab's pre-
posterous "Catatonic Expressionism" flourishes in a "neo-Jacobean
school" (p. 297), he invites comparison of the modern deterioration
to that of "preapocalyptic, death-wishful, sensually fatigued"
seventeenth-century England.

But the seventeenth-century English were complacent, refusing
to worry about the moral, social, and political rot at home as long as
they could deprecate it abroad. *The Courier's Tragedy* is set, properly,
in Italy, which Protestant England regarded as Satan's duchy. According to Salgādo: "Italy was the seed-bed of vice, villainy, and
perversion so vast and various that it was all the right-thinking
sober-minded Englishman could do even to imagine it. It is enough
for one character to say to another, 'Now you are full Italian,' to
indicate his perfection in villainy to the contemporary audience. To
the Protestant fear of Popery was allied, with no apparent sense of
paradox, a popular suspicion of atheism and a Puritan dread of
moral contamination, especially in its sexual aspects."[9] Pynchon
wryly describes the parody-mass the tortured cardinal is forced to
perform—saying "This is my body" with his own severed toe as
host—as "a most anti-clerical scene, perhaps intended as a sop to the
Puritans of the time (a useless gesture since none of them ever went
to plays, regarding them for some reason as immoral)" (p. 69). But
the Puritan attitude toward the play proves important. After the
performance that Oedipa sees, she goes backstage to ask Driblette
about his reference to Trystero. Perhaps out of fear, perhaps out of
contempt for what sounds like scholarly nit-picking, he evades her
questions: " 'You guys, you're like Puritans are about the Bible. So
hung up with words, words' " (p. 79). Later in the novel Emory Bortz
will mention a fellow professor's hypothesis that a pornographic
version of *The Courier's Tragedy* sequestered in the Vatican Library
was a project of the Scurvhamites, "a sect of most pure Puritans"
(p. 155). The idea was presumably to discredit the play (its anti-
Papist elements notwithstanding) and the theatre generally. When
Oedipa wonders why they would do a dirty version of the play, Bortz

explains: " 'As a moral example. They were not fond of the theatre. It was their way of putting the play entirely away from them, into hell. What better way to damn it eternally than to change the actual words. Remember that Puritans were utterly devoted, like literary critics, to the Word' " (p. 156).

Oedipa is also devoted to the Word, for hers is a religious sensibility unmoored to any faith. As more and more of the *disjecta membra* of her world prove to be hieroglyphs on the tomb of Pierce Inverarity, her search for a Rosetta Stone by which to decipher the inscription becomes a quest for the Word, the Logos that is the immanence of divine reason in all things. Often she feels quite close to revelation, as when she senses that she is "at the centre of an odd, religious instant" on first seeing San Narciso from the freeway. In the circuitlike "swirl of houses and streets," she experiences "a hieroglyphic sense of concealed meaning, of an intent to communicate. . . . A revelation . . . trembled just past the threshold of her understanding. Smog hung all around the horizon, the sun on the bright beige countryside was painful; she and the Chevy seemed parked at the centre of an odd, religious instant. As if, on some other frequency, or out of the eye of some whirlwind rotating too slow for her heated skin to feel the centrifugal coolness of, words were being spoken" (pp. 24–25). Wandering in San Francisco later, she gets the same feeling of closeness, feels that the things around her are cryptic "clues" that are compensation "for her having lost the direct, epileptic Word, the cry that might abolish the night" (p. 118).

Like the drifters who sleep in linemen's tents and do not hear the millions of words in transmission around them, Oedipa can never quite tune in on revelation; nevertheless, she knows when she is in the presence of one who has done so. Afflicted with delirium tremens, the old sailor whom she meets has had, briefly and ineffably, experiences richer and more meaningful than any accessible to sober-minded people like Oedipa. "Cammed each night out of that safe furrow the bulk of the city's waking each sunrise again set virtuously to plowing, what rich soils had he turned, what concentric planets uncovered? What voices overheard, flinders of luminescent gods glimpsed among the wallpaper's stained foliage?" (pp. 125–26). How does Oedipa have any inkling of these matters? A seeker after the Word, she becomes attuned to words, to metaphor, paronomasia, and verbal play generally. Thus, embracing the old derelict, "she knew . . . that he suffered DT's. Behind the initials was a metaphor, a delirium tremens, a trembling unfurrowing of the mind's plowshare" (p. 128). *Delirare,* the Latin word meaning "to be crazy," actually means being out *(de)* of the furrow *(lira).* Just as we say that someone is "unhinged"—using a metaphor that is becoming increasingly unconscious—the Romans said that one was "unfurrowed." Pynchon's verbal density here is striking. From the abbreviation (DT's) to the clinical term (delirium tremens) to the original Latin figute *(delirare),* he telescopes a complete etymology ("trembling unfurrowing of the mind's plowshare") and revivifies an ancient metaphor.

Pynchon takes a special interest in the way metaphor manages to express truth that is inaccessible by any other linguistic means. *Metaphor,* the word itself, also has a suggestive etymology; it comes from Greek *pherein* (to bear) and *meta* (across, beyond), and indeed it bears us into the beyond along with Oedipa's old sailor. Normally we think of metaphor as asserting a similarity or identity where "really" none exists. But this formulation misses the mystical properties of metaphor: we often find in yoking things together that the identity asserted is more than verbal. Verbal play, then, is a way of manipulating language to get at the underlying reality that language—by the very fact of its intermediacy—tends to obscure. If language were a clear varnish over the natural grain of things, there would be no misunderstandings, no disagreement between beings endowed with it. But language is radically metaphorical: words "stand for" things, and we cannot, like Swift's Laputian academicians, eliminate error by conversing in things. Since language tends to be euphemistic, it can protect us, or it can simply get in the way. That is why it is useful—if sometimes frightening—to have people who see through language, who manipulate language in puns and metaphors to reveal underlying connections, underlying realities.

If the attitude toward language I have inferred for Pynchon is correct, he has moved beyond the position of Fausto Maijstral in *V.* Fausto defined metaphor as the lie which, in asserting connections and relations between discrete phenomena, gives one the comfort of greater connectedness or cohesiveness in the natural world. The poet, however—metaphor's high priest—sees things too clearly to be comforted: "Living as he does much of the time in a world of metaphor, the poet is always acutely conscious that metaphor has no value apart from its function; that it is a device, an artifice. So that while others may look on the laws of physics as legislation and God as a human form with beard measured in light-years and nebulae for sandals, Fausto's kind are alone with the task of living in a universe of things which simply are, and cloaking that innate mindlessness with comfortable and pious metaphor" (pp. 325–26).

But in *The Crying of Lot 49* Pynchon describes metaphor as something more mysterious and less artificial. Verbal play, moreover, is no longer seen as strictly the province of the poet: "The saint whose water can light lamps, the clairvoyant whose lapse in recall is the breath of God, the true paranoid for whom all is organized in spheres joyful or threatening about the central pulse of himself, the dreamer whose puns probe ancient fetid shafts and tunnels of truth all act in the same special relevance to the word, or whatever the word is there, buffering, to protect us from" (pp. 128–29). *Word* here means symbol—something that represents reality at the same time that it buffers us from it. The words that have generated these speculations on language, "delirium tremens," buffer us from the condition they denote. Like its even less attractive cousin, madness, delirium is not pleasant to experience directly; we can be thankful for the intermediacy of language, for the word or words that buffer us from a too-close contact with the underlying reality. We see how experiencing the condition—unmediated by language—upsets Oedipa. She knows just how harrowing it is because she actually *holds* the old man.

But the contact alone does not account for the intensity of her epiphany. The metaphor she perceives and the pun she presently makes gauge the significance of the old man's experience more accurately than the simple touching and knowing. Pynchon includes punsters among those who act in a "special relevance to the word." The "ancient fetid shafts and tunnels of truth" probed by punning dreamers are, according to Freudian dream-iconography, the uterine and vaginal tunnels through which we passed to our first experience of the world. Freud showed how part of the mechanics of dreams was to compress and distort things our conscious minds dare not confront. While repressed truths are most commonly expressed by means of such devices as projection, cathexis, and symbolization, they can also be rendered as puns. The implication is that language, though it encodes psychic truth, normally functions as an instrument of psychic repression. The more elaborately we use language, the more we "buffer" ourselves from the dyslogistic and reductive physiological facts that, Freud tells us, give rise to all human aspirations and ideals. These ideals—civilization, religion, poetry, the things we dress up most with language—are thus our greatest untruths. As Norman O. Brown says: "It is a shattering experience for anyone seriously committed to the Western traditions of morality and rationality to take a steadfast, unflinching look at what Freud had to say. It is humiliating to be compelled to admit the grossly seamy side of so many grand ideals."[10]

But at the same time that we use language consciously to shore up the illusions that protect us from Freud's shattering physiological truths, we use it unconsciously, in dreams and slips of the tongue, to reveal those truths and our repressed desires. For Pynchon as for Freud, language can be either an instrument of repression or a key to all the mythologies of the mind. If the word is a kind of basic symbol, then a metaphor or pun seems to be a way of short-circuiting language into yielding up a higher than usual level of meaning, *or* it is yet another dodge away from meaning and truth; another remove, a symbol of a symbol. What it is, says Pynchon, depends on one's immediate relation to the verbal play: "The act of metaphor then was a thrust at truth and a lie, depending where you were: inside, safe, or outside, lost" (p. 129). Being a metaphorical insider is simply to perceive the justness of the connection made by the metaphor. If one does not, Pynchon implies, one is "outside" of rather more than a moment's verbal play. Such connections have special epistemological and ontological value. Where Oedipa is concerned, the inside-outside figure can refer to both the metaphor and the mental furrow. She finds herself momentarily outside the furrow, lost, confused. Nevertheless, she makes a punning connection as her mind slips "sidewise, screeching back across grooves of years" (p. 129)—no more bound to metaphorical consistency than Shakespeare, Pynchon turns his furrow into a record groove—until she remembers a previous encounter with the initials that designate the old sailor's condition. The initials in lower case ("dt") are the calculus symbol for—in Pynchon's elegant three-word definition—a "vanishingly small instant" (p. 129). Supralogically, she discovers the common ground between DT's and dt's: "She knew that the sailor had seen worlds no other man had seen if only because there was that high magic to low puns, because DT's must give access to dt's of spectra beyond the known sun, music made purely of Antarctic loneliness and fright" (p. 129). Oedipa's experience is analogous to that of the old man, whose delirium has brought him into contact with infinitesimal yet valuable moments of alien spectra and alien music in "worlds" cold and lonely and frightening. In discovering the Tristero, she too has come into contact with another world—one that ought never to intersect the one in which she normally moves.

The coming together of two utterly disparate worlds is of course exactly what happens in puns and metaphors; their elements have nothing to do with each other—and everything. A pun or metaphor, then, is a paradigm of the kind of "miracle" that Jesus Arrabal, the Mexican revolutionary Oedipa meets in Mazatlán and again in San Francisco, defines as "another world's intrusion into this one" (p. 120). Pynchon intimates that language, too, can reveal the possibility of extra, unexpected orders of being. Oedipa's encounters with words, like her other, more harrowing insights in the search for Tristero, may be interpreted as a sensitizing, a learning to perceive alien "spectra" in her own right. Thus she queries Driblette's onstage reference to Tristero, becomes "just a whiz at pursuing strange words in Jacobean texts" (p. 104), and eventually, discovering the magic and the occasional terror in words, begins probing the mysteries of language itself.

Pynchon's own fascination with these mysteries links him to Barth, Borges, Nabokov, and other contemporary authors who combine a delight in the magic of language with a willingness to experiment with fantasy. Like them, Pynchon has come increasingly to question the traditional realist bias of the novel. His motive in turning from empirical reality to the realm of the supposedly irrational or impossible should be clear by now—he exploits any means to persuade his readers that the world of objective reality is less circumscribed, less understood, and less predictable than they are wont to assume. Important among those who have shaped or influenced his penchant for fantasy are E. M. Forster, with whom he shares a humanist outlook and an acute awareness of the Void, and Charles Dodgson, whose imagination bears no small resemblance to his own. A more personal influence on this aspect of Pynchon's literary personality is his Cornell classmate and kindred spirit, the late Richard Fariña. A surprising number of the fantastic details in Pynchon's work can be traced to encouragement, precedent, or inspiration provided by one or another of this unlikely trio.

The fantastic experiences into which Charles Dodgson plunges the heroine of *Alice's Adventures in Wonderland* and *Through the Looking Glass* have obvious affinities with those of Pynchon's main characters in *The Crying of Lot 49* and *Gravity's Rainbow*. In each of these two novels, as in the Alice books, an innocent tumbles into a strange new world that is utterly unlike anything previously experienced. Absurd experience follows absurd experience, as the innocent encounters a variety of eccentric characters. Periodically the narrative is interrupted for a highly unserious bit of verse or song. The story balances precariously between comedy and nightmare, and of course our dread in the Alice books that we will not be restored to what Northrop Frye calls "the daylight world" is actually realized in Pynchon's versions of these fantasies.

The Crying of Lot 49 might be called *Oedipa in Wonderland*. The harried Yoyodyne mail carrier she sees in the Scope is the White Rabbit she follows, and Pierce Inverarity is the "linearly fading" Cheshire Cat who leaves his sardonic grin behind him. *Gravity's Rainbow*, on the other hand, is like a version of *Through the Looking Glass* in which the protagonist never reaches the eighth square of the chessboard. Tyrone Slothrop, who also goes the way of the Cheshire Cat, meets a number of chessmen characters, including Franz Pökler, one of the Zone's most pawnlike individuals, particularly in his own paranoid view; the redoubtable female pirate Frau Gnahb, a delightfully Dodgsonian queen; and Gerhardt von Göll, known as *Der Springer* because his emblem is a plastic chess knight. As Frau Gnahb says, "He's the white knight of the black market, as I am queen of the coastal trade" (p. 492). Several other characters briefly become metaphoric chessmen at moments of terror, danger, or helplessness. Vaslav Tchitcherine loses his prisoner von Göll, but captures Närrisch, and considers the trade—"a knight for a bishop" (p. 563)—a good one. Pirate Prentice is menaced "bishopwise" in a movie theatre, and Miklos Thanatz, during his days as a D.P. adrift in Lower Saxony, encounters a "Läufer (who is a runner or messenger, but also happens to be the German name for a chess bishop)" (p. 666). "Messenger" is also Dodgson's term for the bishop; his, moreover, is an "Anglo-Saxon Messenger." A broader and more subtle version of the gaming tropes that dominate the narrator's description of the Himmler-Spielsaal at the Casino Hermann Goering, Pynchon's chess imagery contributes to the pervasive atmosphere of fatality and paranoia in *Gravity's Rainbow*.

Through the Looking Glass also provides some of the South-West Africa conceits of both *Gravity's Rainbow* and *V*. As in the transpecular world, everything is backwards in South-West Africa, which operates on "mirror-time" (*V.*, p. 230), and according to "mirror metaphysics" (*Gravity's Rainbow*, p. 101). Backwards, too, is Pynchon's rocket. Like Alice's mirrorland plum cake—first passed around, then sliced—the rocket first explodes, then comes screaming across the sky. But the most intriguing of the Dodgson references comes when Slothrop, aboard the *Anubis,* dreams "about Llandudno, where he spent a rainy furlough once drinking bitter in bed with a tug skipper's daughter. Also where Lewis Carroll wrote that *Alice in Wonderland.* So, they put up a statue of the White Rabbit in Llandudno. White Rabbit's been talking to Slothrop, serious and crucial talk, but on the way up to waking he loses it all, as usual" (p. 468). As *Alice in Wonderland* must be a favorite fantasy among nymphet lovers, Slothrop wakes appropriately to seduction by the "subteen" Bianca. Back at Raoul de la Perlimpinpin's wild party on the Riviera, Slothrop had had eyes for "a girl in a prewar Worth frock and with a face like Tenniel's Alice, same forehead, nose, hair" (p. 247). One recalls that Ralph MacBurgess/Maxwell Rowley-Bugge, in *V.,* was seduced by a ten-year-old called Alice, probably the fantasy name of Victoria Wren. As for the White Rabbit, it may be worth noting that Pynchon's good friend, Richard Fariña, to whom *Gravity's Rainbow* is dedicated, once read the part of the White Rabbit in a small recording company's production of *Alice's Adventures in Wonderland.*[11] Both writers, incidentally, display a whimsical interest in children's literature: Fariña's use of *Winnie-the-Pooh* complements Pynchon's use of the Alice books and German *Märchen.* Fariña died in a motorcycle accident on April 30, 1966, only a month after the publication of *The Crying of Lot 49*—and only two days after the publication of his own novel, *Been Down So Long It Looks Like Up To Me.* In view of the presence of the dead throughout *Gravity's Rainbow,* it may be that Pynchon has briefly introduced his dead friend in Slothrop's dream of the White Rabbit (the poignance of Slothrop's dream-meeting with the dead Tantivy Mucker-Maffick, his one true friend, may also owe something to Pynchon's own loss).

One reason to think Fariña may be in Pynchon's work is that Pynchon is in Fariña's. Fariña left one of the few eyewitness accounts of what Pynchon is like in the flesh. In a sketch entitled "The Monterrey Fair," first published in *Mademoiselle,* and collected in *Long Time Coming And A Long Time Gone,* we see him hunching paranoiacally among the right-wingers at the California fair of the title. Pynchon may also appear in *Been Down So Long.* Mimi Fariña, the author's widow, has remarked that "a lot of people in *Been Down So Long* . . . were modeled after real people and the names had to be changed to protect the innocent, you know."[12] Since the novel is set in 1958, on a campus that is surely Cornell's (the town's name is changed from Ithaca to Athene), and since Pynchon was then a classmate, friend, and fellow rollicker, it stands to reason that he has been included in the book, perhaps as the tall, gangly "quadroon" with the Milnean name of Heffalump. Heffalump and the novel's protagonist, Gnossos Pappadopoulis, engage in a lengthy trivia quiz on radio and comic book personalities, including Hop Harrigan and Tank Tinker, characters mentioned in *Gravity's Rainbow* and *The Crying of Lot 49.*

In reading Fariña's work we find many of the techniques, tastes, prejudices, situations, terms, and obsessions that figure in the work of his friend. In noting these parallels and the implied community of attitudes, we are of course not really considering allusion proper, but in reading the signs of what seems to have been a close friendship we come to a clearer understanding of Pynchon's personality, interests, and attitudes. There were obviously many shared enthusiasms and paranoias, and much intellectual cross-fertilization. Sometimes they even wrote the same way. Though Pynchon has the wider stylistic répertoire, both tend to favor fast-moving prose that often defies conventional grammar, depending on participial phrases that ought to "dangle," but somehow propel instead. Their works are equally studded with catalogues, equations (both had abandoned engineering programs), and parodies of the Mass, not to mention references to movies, the harmonica, the color magenta, aqua regia, black and Latin culture, comics, radio serials, and Vivaldi. While both like music, Fariña's clumsiness with musical allusion reveals, by contrast, Pynchon's acuity. Where Pynchon will make use of, say, highly technical violin-bowing terms with impressive accuracy and authority, Fariña will misremember a term like *"ripieno,"* referring repeatedly, in his story "Harry and the Celluloid Passion," to the *"ribiendo"* of Baroque compositions. In jazz, they shared a contempt for Dave Brubeck, and a liking for Ornette Coleman (if Stanley Edgar Hyman is correct in identifying McClintic Sphere as Coleman).[13] Both delight in comic voices. The Nazi officers, pachucos, Transylvanians, blacks, comic Englishmen, and radio characters like Lamont Cranston who stalk through Pynchon's fiction may have been inspired by Fariña's répertoire of such voices, which his sister-in-law, Joan Baez, describes in her introduction to the *Long Time Coming* collection. Both loved comedy, and both were fascinated by death. Though Fariña was often, in his wife's term, very "deathy," he did not live long enough for his youthful, Hamlet-like brooding on mortality to mature into real nihilism. Perhaps in time, like his friend, he would have tempered nihilism with something like mysticism and discovered in fantasy and the heartening vistas of the imagination that physics is metaphor, not law. Pynchon's own transition from nihilist to quasi-mystic may in a small way owe something to E. M. Forster, whom I have often mentioned in the course of this study. Forster himself never made the transition to mysticism, though the closing pages of *A Passage to India* are suggestive. He did, however, make high claims for the "holiness of the heart's affections," and he did delight in fantasy, a mode which he defends—albeit a little diffidently—in his *Aspects of the Novel*. Forster seldom wrote about science, but implicit in his work is the kind of scientifically informed outlook set forth in Bertrand Russell's famous essay, "A Free Man's Worship." The Void that haunts Pynchon haunts Forster as well, as is apparent in the programmatic treatment of Beethoven's Fifth Symphony in *Howards End* and in the episode at the Malabar Caves in *A Passage to India*. Mrs. Moore's experience in the caves could almost have inspired Oedipa Maas's epiphany in Mexico City.

Forster and Pynchon have a number of other things in common as well. Both, for example, seem to know and love Florence, Alexandria, and the Mediterranean generally. But they are closest in their delight in allusion, and they exhibit numerous similarities of taste. Both like painting, especially Renaissance painting, and opera, especially Wagner. Pynchon's rendering of theatre scenes like the performance of *Manon Lescaut* in "Under the Rose" and the première of the *Rite of Spring* in *V.* should be compared to the uproarious performance of *Lucia di Lammermoor* in *Where Angels Fear to Tread*. Their allusions serve them in similar ways. The moral and aesthetic dialectic Forster adumbrates by playing Giotto off against Alessio di Baldovinetti in *A Room with a View* differs very little from the Beethoven-Rossini antithesis in *Gravity's Rainbow*.

The most concrete evidence of Pynchon's interest in Forster, however, comes in a somewhat unexpected way. Woven into *Gravity's Rainbow* are oblique allusions to nearly all of Forster's *Collected Tales*. (One is reminded of the page in *Finnegans Wake* where Joyce manages to cite the title of each of the stories in *Dubliners*.) In the tales Forster, like Pynchon, plays with metamorphosis ("Other Kingdom"), nature spirits ("The Story of a Panic"), the forbidding future ("The Machine Stops"), the Other Side ("The Other Side of the Hedge"), pre-Christian atavism ("The Story of the Siren"), and rainbow symbolism ("The Celestial Omnibus").

In the first of the *Collected Tales*, "The Story of a Panic," a group of English tourists wander into the invisible presence of "the Great God Pan" and with one mind suddenly scatter, victims of unreasoning panic. Pynchon contrasts this traditional kind of panic to what one feels in the eerie *Mittelwerke* at Nordhausen: "it was always easy, in open and lonely places, to be visited by Panic wilderness fear, but these are the urban fantods here" (p. 303). While Pynchon would not have had to get his Pan lore from Forster, he at least shares the British author's fascination with the "goat god," who numbers among his intimates Katje Borgesius (pp. 656–57) and Geli Tripping (pp. 720–21). Forster may also contribute to Slothrop's experience at the crossroads, where he tunes in to the Other Side. "Serial time" does not exist on the Other Side, Pynchon remarks, because "events are all there in the same eternal moment" (p. 624). While "The Eternal Moment" is the title of another Forster short story, Slothrop's extrasensory "listening in" is more closely associated with the Forster story entitled "The Other Side of the Hedge," whose main character also pauses by the roadside and ends up discovering a completely different and richer order of experience. A fable about time, age, and the fallacy of "progress," the story presents modern life as an endless, meaningless trek along a dusty road bordered by a hedge. The point is to press on, to cover distance, though no one has any idea where the road actually leads. The main character cuts through the hedge beside the road and finds himself in a beautiful and timeless landscape—one that does not "go anywhere." The people in this Land of Cockaigne show him that his road begins here, at gates of ivory, and ends here, at gates of horn. The implications are plain, and parallel those of Slothrop's experience. Both Pynchon and Forster question the Western-capitalist ethic of progress.

Though Pynchon dispenses with the explicitly Virgilian mythology, he also makes use of metaphorical gates, as in Roger Mexico's song, "They took us at the gates of green return" (p. 627), or in the description of Gottfried's emotions during his last days:

> As man and woman, coupled, are shaken to the teeth at their approaches to the gates of life, hasn't he also felt more, worshipfully more past these arrangements for penetration, the style, garments of flaying without passion, sheer hosiery perishable as the skin of any snake, custom manacles and chains to stand for the bondage he feels in his heart . . . all become theatre as he approaches the gates of that Other

Kingdom, felt the white gigantic muzzles somewhere inside, expressionless beasts frozen white, pushing him away, the crust and mantle hum of mystery so beyond his poor hearing. (p. 722)

Pynchon here envisages antithetical portals—gates of life (approached by heterosexual coupling) and gates of death (approached by homosexual coupling)—that recall Virgil's gates for true dreams and false dreams and Forster's for reality and illusion. Gottfried approaches the gates of death in a double sense: as a homosexual and as the victim of Blicero's murderous experiment. But nothing in Pynchon is that straightforward, least of all mortality itself. More than an Eliotic epithet for death, "Other Kingdom" is also the title of another Forster short story in which, metamorphosed into a hamadryad, a young woman crosses over into another "kingdom" on a different existential plane, leaving behind a staid, stale, and exitless milieu. Again, Pynchon eschews the mythological machinery; but the imagined possibilities of an otherwordly kingdom—whether Forster's or Eliot's—are very much part of his program.

Forster wanted to criticize various kinds of religious, social, and cultural stuffiness with his mythological fantasies. Pynchon, who wants to criticize *perceptual* stuffiness, does not need the mythology because he finds in modern science a more trenchant critical tool. Moreover, science is for Pynchon both a destroyer and a creator of transcendental systems, whereas for a writer of Forster's generation it was only a destroyer. Thus even Thomas Hardy—whose works are permeated with transcendence-bludgeoning science—occasionally turns to mythology, as when he makes the young Sue Bridehead express her spiritual discontent by keeping statues of Venus and Apollo. Unable to make of their mythological fantasies anything substantial, writers like Hardy and Forster had little more than imagination to offer as an alternative to the stifling and misguided pieties of their times. But Pynchon offers imagination that somehow no longer seems fantastic, imagination endorsed as it were by the very science it once sought to circumvent, transcend, or deny.

Like Hardy, Pynchon sometimes bypasses not only Christianity but also the familiar mythologies of Bullfinch to invoke the nameless, earth-oriented cults that preceded civilized memory. Still, the initial inspiration can come from Forster, as in the account of Blicero's last days, when, according to Miklos Thanatz, he reverted to some ancestral version of himself, screamed at the sky, sat hours in a rigid trance, with his eyes rolled clear up into his head. . . . White blank ovals, the eyes of a statue, with the gray rain behind them. He had left 1945, wired his nerves back into the pre-Christian earth we fled across, into the Urstoff of the primitive German, God's poorest and most panicked creature. You and I perhaps have become over the generations so Christianized, so enfeebled by Gesellschaft and its celebrated "Contract," which never did exist, that we, even we, are appalled at reversions like that. But deep, out of its silence, the Urstoff wakes, and sings. (p. 465)

The Forster tale behind this passage is "The Story of the Siren." Like the atavistic Blicero, the Siren is a manifestation of pre-Christian truth. Those who see the Siren, deep in the blue waters of Sicily, are about as good for ordinary human intercourse as Blicero. They are terribly enlightened. One who has seen the Siren is described as "unhappy because he knew everything. Every living thing made him unhappy because he knew it would die."[14] But while knowledge of the Siren begins with knowledge of death and the Void, it culminates in the wisdom and repudiation of cant that come with knowing the truth, however grim. Thus Forster's story emphasizes the positive, humanistic aspect of Sirenic truth; he even prophesied a Sirenic apocalypse. As he described it in his introduction to Giuseppe di Lampedusa's "The Professor and the Mermaid" years later, the Siren "was to stay hidden until ritually summoned, when she would rise to the surface, sing, destroy silence, primness, and cruelty, and save the world."[15] The singing of the Siren would destroy a parvenu order (Christianity), to restore the plainer and harder one that preceded it. The Siren represents the same pre-Christian *Urstoff* (literally, "primary matter") into which Blicero had "wired his nerves." Blicero took his name, we recall, from the one the ancient, pre-Christian Germans gave to death. Death, then, is his "kingdom," and Greta von Erdmann sees it mapped in his eyes (p. 670). Wired into the *Urstoff*, Blicero becomes Sirenic, a terrible icon of mortality, and stripped, even, of Forster's tempering humanism. His launching of the 00000 is an act whose apocalyptic ramifications are clear enough, but the association of that act with Forster's "Story of the Siren" provides it with another overtone, another resonant suggestion regarding the magnitude of what takes place there on the Lüneburg Heath.

Forster's short stories, like Pynchon's writings, alternate between the hard truths of mortality and the boundless possibilities of imagination. Forster critiques the things with which we delude ourselves—religion, progress, art, education, society. His antidotes to human folly—tolerance, simplicity, "the holiness of the heart's affections"—are, in the stories, irradiated by a transforming imagination. Indeed, when a young woman escapes a stifling social situation by turning into a tree, or when "silence and primness" are given the lie by a being out of Greek mythology, Forster seems to be saying that imagination is itself the most powerful thing we have to combat stupidity, pretense, self-delusion, and the "exitlessness" of modern life that distresses Oedipa Maas. Pynchon might agree, for imagination is the most salient feature of his own talent. It is his forte, and he learns from artists like Forster, Remedios Varo, Anton Webern, and—as will be seen presently—Rainer Maria Rilke—how to use it to subvert graceless empiricism and hint at rich new horizons for humanity. Bringing this transforming imagination to the shores of modern science, he launches it, knowing—if only because today's tachyons will be tomorrow's atomies—that its sails will fill.

Pynchon's imagination and his indulgence of it in the fantasy elements of his fiction enable him to gainsay death itself, the most graceless empirical fact of all. Pynchon sees death, like outer space, as part of the realm of possibility; it was suggested in the last chapter that certain musical allusions, like the twelve-tone song whose notes fall apart like dead proteins, were associated with not only death's horror, but also its promise of transformation. Many of Pynchon's literary allusions also provide reflections on death: T. S. Eliot, Emily Dickinson, Randall Jarrell, Keats, Hemingway, and German *Märchen* all contribute to the imagery of mortality in *Gravity's Rainbow*. But none contributes as much as Rilke. Pynchon cites his work more often than that of any other literary figure, nor does he have to look hard to find reflections on mortality in the work of this poet who was obsessed with death.

Pynchon's favorite poems by Rilke seem to be the *Sonnets to Orpheus,* inspired, like Donne's *Anniversaries,* by the death of a young girl, and the Tenth of the *Duino Elegies,* which describes the death and transfiguration of a youth. Rilke believed that life's whole point was to be found in death and its unknowable transformations. C. F. MacIntyre, one of his translators, uses words from the Ninth Elegy to explain: "We must give ourselves confidently to earth's 'sacred revelation . . . intimate death.' " The Tenth Elegy shows how man comes to understand pain at the end of his life. Rilke saw the pain and suffering of earthly existence as something to be transformed into art; this was, at least for him, the only suitable preparation for death. Sorrow, then, should be, in MacIntyre's words, "a stimulus for praise."[16]

The Tenth Elegy, in which death is most sternly and beautifully imagined, appears first in *Gravity's Rainbow* in the thoughts of Weissmann, who had taken the *Duino Elegies* with him to South-West Africa as a young man, there to marvel at constellations as strange and new as those described in the poem. His quoting it early in the novel foreshadows his launching of Gottfried at the end, for it describes, in Pynchon's words, the leaving behind of life by a "newly dead youth," embracing his Lament, his last link leaving now even her marginally human touch forever, climbing all alone, up and up into the mountains of primal Pain" (p. 98). Pynchon paraphrases the actual words of Rilke here: *"Einsam steigt er dahin, in die Berge des Ur-Leids."* He cites the next line in both German and English: *"Und nicht einmal sein Schritt klingt aus dem tonlosen Los. . . . And not once does his step ring from the soundless Destiny"* (p. 98). When Blicero contemplates these lines early in the book, he sees himself as the dead youth and sees his coming annihilation in the oven he will be pushed into by his captive Hänsel and Gretel (Gottfried and Katje) as his "Destiny." But the poem comes ultimately to comment on the passage into some strange new order of experience by Gottfried, who also has a last "link" to earthly life—Blicero's one-way radio hookup—during his "ascent" toward a destiny that is "soundless" because supersonic. In a larger sense, however, the poem provides a suggestive eulogy for all the characters of *Gravity's Rainbow* who die or fade away from the present, only to continue making appearances in the book: Peter Sachsa, Brigadier Pudding, Tantivy Mucker-Maffick, Walter Rathenau, Sir Charles Dodson-Truck, Lyle Bland, and Tyrone Slothrop.

When Rilke's poetry is not being quoted directly, it seems to be influencing Pynchon's imagery indirectly. Some of Pynchon's allusions are ambiguous, and perhaps conflated with references to other sources. Where, for example, does Pynchon get his "Riders," those mysterious and minatory entities in the Zone's skies? The alien constellations seen in the Tenth Elegy's "mountains of primal pain" into which the dead youth ascends include one called *Der Reiter,* to be sure, but Pynchon's Riders could also come from Tolkien, whose hobbits are menaced by superhuman "Dark Riders," or from Ernest

Hemingway, whose character Harry Street (the moribund and half-delirious writer in "The Snows of Kilimanjaro") sees death as pairs of bicycle-riding policemen. Indeed, a portentous "Bicycle Rider in the Sky" (p. 501), apparently formed by two radial explosions on the horizon, appears to Slothrop over Peenemünde's demolished facilities, but there may be another indirect allusion to Rilke when the spokes of the Rider's wheels later prove to be windmill vanes (p. 509). Windmills in *Gravity's Rainbow* tend to be variations on a single windmill called "The Angel." A looming presence in several scenes, "The Angel" is meant to remind us of the secular Angels in Rilke that dispassionately monitor the doings of humans. (Pynchon introduces one of these in actuality, of course, during the bombing of Lübeck by the British.) Pynchon's emphasis on the great windmill known as "The Angel" guarantees that any windmill on the horizon will be perceived as a mysterious and monitory presence. But part of the importance of windmills lies in the contrast they provide, in their relationship with the environment, to the A4 rocket. In a simple ecological way, a windmill harnesses a natural force and converts it into work—pumping water, grinding grain, or generating electricity. Thus it surrenders itself to the natural force which defines it, unlike the rocket, which must continually defy both that natural force—it even has to be tested in "wind tunnels"—and that other all-important natural force, gravity. Another important aspect of the windmill stems from its "mandalic" shape in the landscape: its cruciform vanes and the circle they describe in turning are similar to the symbolic designs used as aids to meditation in certain Eastern religions.

From the windmill and the A4 to the carbon atom, with its four valences, the fourfold mandala and other more or less mythic quaternities proliferate in *Gravity's Rainbow;* indeed, as Sir Thomas Browne demonstrated with the quincunx centuries before Jung, mandalas are everywhere in both nature and human culture. But while circles and quaternities occur commonly enough in literature and mythology, Pynchon probably does get his mandala lore from the theories of Jung, who claimed that mandalas inhere in a "collective unconscious," a repository of mythic symbols for the whole human race. Jung defined the mandala as an archetypal emblem of now the universe, now the self, now the deity, and the mandalas of *Gravity's Rainbow* run the full gamut of possible referents. To gauge the importance of mandalas in Pynchon's novel, one needs to consider not only windmills and the A4, but also Slothrop's KEZVH insignia, the ellipse at Peenemünde's Test Stand VII, Herero villages, and the *Raketen-Stadt,* all of which partake of the mystical configuration. An examination can be conducted to best advantage by ordering the discussion around Pynchon's mandalic Holy City, an idealized version of the community of scientists and technicians who lived and worked first at Peenemünde during the war, then in Huntsville, Alabama—a town whose chamber-of-commerce name happens in fact to be "Rocket City." Imagined visually, the author's apotheosized, numinous City owes a good deal to futuristic movies of the twenties and thirties, like *Metropolis,* its American imitation *Just Imagine,* and the H. G. Wells-inspired *Things to Come.* Indeed, one description sounds like the famous passage from "Locksley Hall" updated by Hollywood: "It's a giant factory-state here, a City of the Future full of extrapolated 1930s swoop-facaded and balconied skyscrapers, lean chrome caryatids with bobbed hairdos, classy airships of all descriptions drifting in the boom and hush of the city abysses, golden lovelies sunning in roof-gardens and turning to wave as you pass. It is the Raketen-Stadt" (p. 674). The *Raketen-Stadt* becomes more than a mere city of the future, however; it becomes a holy city in the mold of the New Jerusalem or City of God. The *locus classicus* of the holy city topos being the Book of Revelation, it is, appropriately, in the growing atmosphere of apocalypse towards the end of *Gravity's Rainbow* that the fantastic Rocket City descriptions occur. "So yes yes this is a scholasticism here, Rocket state-cosmology" (p. 726).

As usual with holy city archetypes, the *Raketen-Stadt* belongs to all time. It exists in the past as well as in the future, and the narrator even describes a Daguerreotype of the city dating from 1856. The photograph shows "the ceremonial City, fourfold as expected, an eerie precision to all lines and shadings architectural and human, built in mandalic form like a Herero village" (p. 725). The comparison refers to the *Schwarzkommando* Andreas Orukambe's interpretation of the "KEZVH" insignia—itself a mandala—found by Slothrop. The KEZVH mandala was "adapted from insignia the German troopers wore in South-West Africa when they came in 1904 to crush the Herero rebellion." The five letters on it represent, among other things, "the five positions of the launching switch in the A4 control car" (p. 361). Andreas explains that Herero villages were laid out in the same quartered circle. Taking the mandala from Slothrop,

Andreas sets it on the ground, turns it till the K points northwest. "Klar," touching each letter, "Entlüftung, these are the female letters. North letters. In our villages the women lived in huts on the northern half of the circle, the men on the south. The village itself was a mandala. Klar is fertilization and birth, Entlüftung is the breath, the soul. Zündung and Vorstufe are the male signs, the activities, fire and preparation for building. And in the center, here, Hauptstufe. It is the pen where we keep the sacred cattle. The souls of the ancestors. All the same here. Birth, soul, fire, building. Male and female, together." (p. 563)

Viewed from above or below, with the four fins quartering the circle of its fuselage, the A4 rocket which the deracinated Herero come to serve is the same mandala. As Andreas says, "You can see how we might feel it speak to us, even if we don't set one up on its fins and worship it."

If we recall at this point that a mandala can be an emblem of the self, and note, further, that its centre can represent a psychological goal—"wholeness"—that every human mind seeks to attain, we can take the interpretation of the KEZVH insignia a step farther. For the *Schwarzkommando*, "self" is by definition pluralistic, tribal. The KEZVH mandala symbolizes the tribal self or identity which they attempt to express or reclaim by acting out a version of the Kabbalistic apocalypse—the returning of the pieces of the universal smashed vessel to a centre for assembly. The vessel's fragments are represented not only by the components of the 00001, of course, but also by the *Schwarzkommando* themselves. For Slothrop, on the other hand, the KEZVH insignia symbolizes the individual self. He suffers, in Pynchon's Jungian term, from being "uncentered." He travels in a giant circle on the map of Europe: from London, to the Riviera, to Zurich, to Geneva, to Zurich, to Nordhausen, to the Brocken, to Berlin, to Potsdam, to "Bad Karma" (perhaps Bad Freienwald), to Swinemünde, to Peenemünde, to Swinemünde, to Stralsund, to "south of Rostock," to "near Wismar," to Cuxhaven. Ghostlike, he subsequently appears to Pig Bodine at the Chicago Bar in Berlin. A page later, the narrator mentions that there may be "a last photograph" of Slothrop "on the only record album ever put out by The Fool, an English rock group—seven musicians posed, in the arrogant style of the early Stones, near an old rocket-bomb site, out in the East End, or South of the River" (p. 742). Slothrop has, then, come full circle, back to London, where the falling rockets started it all. He never approaches his centre, which is the Lüneburg Heath, where the 00000 was fired. He also circles to the *right,* which Jung describes as the direction (in dream and ritual) symbolic of consciousness, rather than to the *left,* which is the direction of the unconscious[17] (into which he must penetrate if he is ever to understand what was done to him in infancy). When Slothrop does penetrate a "Holy Center" at Peenemünde's "ceremonial plexus," nothing happens, and the narrator apologizes to the local numina: "Forgive the fist that doesn't tighten in his chest, the heart that can't stiffen in any greeting" (p. 510). But the narrator has already dismissed Slothrop's chances for attaining his centre. Although "Holy-Center-Approaching is soon to be the number one Zonal pastime . . . tankers the like of . . . Slothrop here will have already been weeded out" (p. 508).

The centre being so difficult of attainment, a mandala's "quaternity," or fourfold division, tends to be its most prominent or at least tangible feature. The concept of the mandala may be so compelling because quaternities have in all cultures been highly mythic. There are four gospels, four corners of the earth, four seasons, four horsemen of the apocalypse, four letters in the name of God (the Tetragrammaton), and four symbols associated with the quest for the Holy Grail—lance, cup, sword, dish. These last were, according to Jessie L. Weston, absorbed into the four suits of that repository of the Hermetic tradition, the Tarot deck (which Pynchon uses). Moreover, the quaternity is part of the traditional symbolism of the New Jerusalem, according to Northrop Frye: "In apocalyptic symbolism we have the 'waters of life,' the fourfold river of Eden which reappears in the City of God."[18] Thus it is proper that the *Raketen-Stadt* be documented in the past (the 1856 Daguerreotype) as well as in the future. Pynchon's mythopoetical range here embraces the Alpha and the Omega, for the fourfold aspect of the *Raketen-Stadt* links it to the Eden of Genesis and the New Jerusalem of Revelation.

Pynchon's other mythic cities, Happyville and *Die Leid-Stadt,* should be included in a consideration of this archetype's function in the novel. Happyville is Pynchon's imaginary opposite to Rilke's City of Pain, described in the Tenth of the *Duino Elegies.* In a typical paranoid fantasy, a "pointsman" is imagined who determines which place one goes to: "He is the pointsman. He is called that because he throws the lever that changes the points. And we go to Happyville instead of to Pain City. Or 'Der Leid-Stadt,'[19] that's what the Germans call it. There is a mean poem about the Leid-Stadt, by a German man named Mr. Rilke" (p. 644). Neither place would be very attractive. "Happyville" has a meretricious sound to it, and *Die Leid-Stadt*, in Rilke's poem, is a place consecrated to the propagation of money. But outside this ugly place begins the finer, truer "Land of Lamentation," the country through which the newly dead, escorted by personified "Laments," pass to the "mountains of primal pain." Pynchon seems to share Rilke's contempt for simple-minded conceptions of immortality. As we have seen, Pynchon associates Rilke's "newly dead youth" with Gottfried, who also makes an ascent, leaving earthly life more and more irrevocably behind him. The afterlife to which Gottfried and Rilke's youth journey, while not necessarily more pleasant than the choiring eternity of Christianity, is something vastly more mysterious and even less knowable to the living.

Gottfried's death, or at least the preparation for it, is imagined as a sexual experience, for the launching of the 00000 will be an insemination of space itself. Thus Gottfried's confinement in the rocket is a ranging of sexual symbols; erect penis, erect candle, erect flesh—even, as Miklos Thanatz recalls, erect bystanders (p. 465). Though paradoxically womblike, the rocket, too, is phallic. Gottfried's limbs writhe "among the fuel, oxidizer, live-steam lines, thrust frame, compressed air battery, exhaust elbow, decomposer, tanks, vents, valves." Gottfried is advised that "one of these values, one test point, one pressure switch is the right one, the true clitoris, routed directly into the nervous system of the 00000" (p. 751). This scene had been anticipated three hundred pages previously, when Slothrop felt himself *"inside his own cock. . . .* His arms and legs it seems *woven* among vessels and ducts, his sperm roaring louder and louder, getting ready to erupt, somewhere below his feet . . . maroon and evening cuntlight reaches him in a single ray through the opening at the top, refracted through the clear juices up around him. He is enclosed. Everything is about to come, come incredibly, and he's helpless here in this exploding *emprise* . . . red flesh echoing . . . an extraordinary sense of *waiting to rise.* (p. 470)

One accounts for Slothrop's experience as another manifestation of his affinity with the rocket and with Imipolex G, which enshrouds Gottfried—whose sister-self, Bianca, Slothrop is making love to here. More important, though, is the implied association of Rocketman and Rocketboy, an association suggesting that Slothrop's fate is to be seen as somehow complementary to Gottfried's. Slothrop, too, resembles Rilke's youth. Gottfried, at death, travels figuratively into *die*

Berge des Ur-Leids, but Slothrop ascends literally into the mountains, where he commences a modulation out of "self," beyond "identity," as the narrator intones over him the moving lines from the twenty-ninth of Rilke's *Sonnets to Orpheus:* "And though Earthliness forget you, / To the stilled Earth say: I flow. / To the rushing water speak: I am." Playing his harmonica by the stream that has suggested these lines, Slothrop "is closer to being a spiritual medium than he's been yet" (p. 622), and presently, spread-eagled so that he is himself a mandala, he becomes that "spiritual medium," and has the experience by the crossroads—familiar to us by now—in which he listens in to the Other Side.

Slothrop finds mandalas, sees mandalas in the sky and all around him, and becomes a mandala himself. Along with the *Raketen-Stadt*—a resident of which Slothrop imagines himself, *qua* comic book hero—mandalas are part of a spiritual or mythic panoply that Pynchon rather renovates than revivifies. For Pynchon is at fiction's leading edge: his contemporary, Robert Coover, has compared the fictionist of Pynchon's generation to the novel's creator, Cervantes, who turned the fictive art of his time inside out to demolish an outmoded art form, the quest-romance, and establish a major new one. Coover's apostrophe to Cervantes applies as well to Pynchon, and I quote it here because it suggests that we are at the beginning of a whole new literary era—as readers were centuries ago when Don Quixote, with his heteroclite but ultimately cogent notions about reality and illusion, rode into their imaginations:

> Your stories ... exemplified the dual nature of all good narrative art: they struggled against the unconscious mythic residue in human life and sought to synthesize the unsynthesizable, sallied forth against adolescent thought-modes and exhausted art forms, and returned home with new complexities. In fact, your creation of a synthesis between poetic analogy and literal history (not to mention reality and illusion, sanity and madness, the erotic and the ludicrous, the visionary and the scatological) gave birth to the Novel— perhaps above all else your works were exemplars of a revolution in narrative fiction, a revolution which governs us—not unlike the way you found yourself abused by the conventions of the Romance—to this very day.[20]

The point here is that certain of our modern writers—those who, like Pynchon, wrench most violently the old forms—may though destroying the novel as we know it be erecting something as revolutionary and splendid as the genre shaped by Cervantes. *Gravity's Rainbow* could well be the *Don Quixote* of the new era. Pynchon also resembles Cervantes in that he has created a new, parodic literature of the quest. Tyrone Slothrop seems capable of *being* the rocket he seeks, but never of *finding* it. Like Oedipa Maas, Slothrop pursues a chimerical grail, impossible to obtain. Even though the object of his quest—like the object of Herbert Stencil's—is a tangible entity, he cannot close with it. Stencil "approached and avoided," but Slothrop seems to be following an ignis fatuus that retreats before him—and his journey is as circular as Winnie-the-Pooh's. Pynchon's other questers also travel in circles. Stencil finally makes it to Malta, only to yo yo off again; it seems likely he will eventually return, moth to candle, for further irresolute probings. Oedipa Maas, fascinated by circuitry, and reminded, as she gazes down on the orderly tracts of San Narciso from the freeway, of the circuits she has seen in transistor radios, winds up literally spinning, "pivoting on one stacked heel" (p. 177), and possibly "assumed full circle into some paranoia" (p. 182). Even Kinneret, her home, is Hebrew for *circuit*.

The quest, however circular, would seem to be the single indispensable ingredient in Pynchon's books. In each of the novels, that which is quested for is surrounded by a wealth of historical and mythopoeic material that informs the quest with larger symbolic meanings. The enigmatic V. becomes an emblem of Western civilization; her gradual deterioration, progressing from the nineteenth century into modern times, parallels the decline of the West. In *The Crying of Lot 49* Oedipa Maas sifts the detritus of a decaying culture to probe the failure of the American Dream. In *Gravity's Rainbow* Tyrone Slothrop quests in a landscape blasted by the West's most destructive conflict; he seeks a key to his own identity in a piece of "hardware" that is an earnest of either man's annihilation or his apotheosis.

Pynchon's novels have behind them a literary quest tradition extending from *Oedipus Rex* to modern detective novels. In earlier quest literature, the quest's success was a real possiblity: Oedipus, Pericles, Percival, and Sam Spade all find what they are looking for. The grail quests of King Arthur's Knights of the Round Table were undertaken with some certainty of the existence and value of that which was sought. The Waste Land to be redeemed, moreover, was local, not cosmic. Pynchon's quests, on the other hand, take place in a secular age, an age that has lost the community of values that gave meaning to the quest and its literary treatment in the past. Pynchon's quester must search for a grail that is artificial, arbitrary, and perhaps wholly without relevance to the more terrible Waste Land to be redeemed in the modern age. But if the value of the grail seems problematic, the quest itself continues to seem worthwhile, because it is in the nature of questing to be purposive, if only in appearance. Once we are fooled into attaching value to the quest, we tend to attach value to its object as well, however factitious; thus the arbitrary grail and the spurious quest lend each other mutual support. As the quest goes on, the grail surrogate begins to take on numinous qualities, and the quest becomes the seeking of a new revelation, "the cry that would abolish the night" (*The Crying of Lot 49,* p. 118).

A temporary value system results, but one which will support a fairly imposing literary edifice. Pynchon's solution to the problem of making literature in the modern age is a synthesis of the myth-making approaches of Faulkner, Yeats, and Eliot. At the same time that he revives the holy grail myth that served Eliot, he creates an altogether new myth, as Yeats did in *A Vision.* But where Yeats made schemata, Pynchon makes labyrinths. The distinction may surprise us, inasmuch as Yeats despised and ignored modern science, while Pynchon makes it an integral part of his mythos. Notwithstanding the attention to science, however, Pynchon's myth derives much of its potency from a judicious lack of clarity in its presentation. Its appeal lies in the fact that the reader is forced to encounter it in the half-light of a studied ambiguity: hence the labyrinthine plots and the deliberate obscurantism.

Obviously if the myth is brought too sharply into focus—Yeats's mistake—it loses the powerful appeal of ambiguity. This is the failing of *V.,* in which the quest is more or less successful—even if Herbert Stencil prefers carrying on as if it were not. By being successful it loses much of its mystery and consequently much of its potential as myth; when the mystery is solved, we end up with only a clever detective story. In *V.*'s more sophisticated sequels, the never-successful work of the detective-quester stands more convincingly for the search that man has always engaged in: the attempt to probe reality and to understand himself.

Since Pynchon limns his quest in the most resonant terms in *Gravity's Rainbow,* with continual attention to and awareness of the literary-quest tradition, it will be most instructive and useful to examine that book's quest trappings in some detail. Replete with knights errant, vigils, monsters, grails, enchanted castles, sorcerers. tyrants, and damsels in distress, the book seems at times closer to Chrétien de Troyes or Wolfram von Eschenbach than to even so experimental a post-Flaubertian novelist as Joyce. If knights-errant be defined as military men who operate on their own, Pynchon's tale is full of them, with Tchitcherine and Marvy the prime examples. Even Pointsman sees himself as a Tannhäuser or Theseus (pp. 88, 142). Slothrop, however, plays the knightly hero most consistently. Though occasionally making common cause with other individuals or groups, he is essentially alone in his quest. Like knights of old, he undergoes the customary vigil when he spends the night at the grave of Laszlo Jamf. His adventures are recorded by "chroniclers." As the women in the grail romances found Lancelot, Gawain, Tristan, and Perceval irresistible, so their sisters in London, on the Riviera, and in the Zone seem positively to dote on Slothrop. He in turn treats them chivalrously, even rescuing one—Katje—from the traditional monster (Octopus Grigori). He also becomes entangled with a predatory woman (Margherita von Erdmann), as did Lancelot, Tristan, and Tannhäuser. He suffers at the hands of a powerful sorcerer (Jamf), defies a tyrant (Pointsman), outwits an evil knight (Marvy), and rescues a fellow "knight" (von Göll) held in thrall by Tchitcherine. He aids the weak and the oppressed, including Squalidozzi, the *Schwarzkommando,* little Ludwig, and, *qua* Plechazunga, a whole townful of people beset by diminutive Vikings. (Like Tristan of Lyonesse a master of disguise, he appears not only as the Pig Hero, but also as Ian Scuffling, as a "zootster," as a Soviet intelligence operative, and of course as Rocketman.) Unlikely as it may seem, Slothrop also fits the type of Faust, the questing knight as intellectual. Having mastered all available data on the A4 rocket during his training on the Riviera, Slothrop commands the very pinnacle of contemporary science. As unsatisfied as the legendary scholar, he sets out to learn more, to the peril of his "personal density" (p. 509), if not his soul. He even dallies, as Faust did, with a comely witch on the Brocken.

But Slothrop seems a lovably deluded Don Quixote as well, and the reader knows, the knightly window dressing notwithstanding, that "it's all theatre"—that no quest will redeem the modern Waste Land, particularly not one as contrived as Slothrop's. There is a good deal of ambivalence and even mockery about Slothrop's role, and about that which he seeks: "The Schwarzgerät is no Grail, Ace, that's not what the G in Imipolex G stands for. And you are no knightly hero" (p. 364). Not that Slothrop is alone in his naïveté and gullibility in these matters. Everyone seems to have his personal grail, which is also his personal delusion. Pointsman seeks the Nobel Prize, and Joseph Ombindi, of the *Schwarzkommando,* believes in the "old Tribal unity" of the Herero in an earlier era of cultural innocence: "He will profess and proclaim it, as an image of a grail slipping through the room, radiant, though the jokers around the table be sneaking Whoopee Cushions into the Siege Perilous, under the very descending arse of the grailseeker, though the grails themselves come in plastic these years, a dime a dozen, penny a gross, still Ombindi, at times self-conned as any Christian, praises and prophesies that era of innocence he just missed living in" (p. 321). The passage reveals a fragmentation of creeds and a proliferation of phony relics. The holy things of old are cheapened and, finally, secularized. An indiscriminately reproduced grail of plastic—the very stuff of vulgarity—can hardly beckon or reassure the faithful. It can have little spiritual efficacy.

The original grail derived its potency from the precious fluid it had contained, the Eucharistic wine, transubstantiated to Christ's blood. The Eucharist, after all, began as a blood sacrifice. In the Zone there is only one genuine blood vehicle, one relic unvitiated by the waning of the creed that gives it meaning. This is the fragment of Pig Bodine's undershirt, soaked in the blood of the Counterforce's adopted martyr, John Dillinger, after federal agents ambushed him outside Chicago's Biograph Theatre in 1934. In his last appearance in the book, Slothrop, who has faded to a voiceless presence, receives the fragment from Bodine. "One of the few who can still see Slothrop as any sort of integral creature any more," Bodine proffers the blood sacrifice like that other sailor, Odysseus, pouring out blood for the shade of Tiresias in the Underworld. But the blood seems not to revive Slothrop; he continues to fade. We derive hope only from the promise implicit in the existence of a martyr and a Counterforce.

Margherita von Erdmann experiences an even more striking illustration of Eucharistic desuetude and ineffectuality, one foreshadowed by the comment on Joseph Ombindi's grail-seeking: "the grails themselves come in plastic these years." Blicero takes her to "the Castle"—a petrochemicals plant, the modern version of the enchanted castle of Klingsor, the sorcerer of the Perceval story. A holy relic stolen by evil forces is standard in quest literature, and just as Klingsor had possessed himself of the sacred lance, the rulers of "the Castle" smugly display the relic they have preempted and degraded: "a heavy chalice of methyl methacrylate, a replica of the Sangraal" (p. 487). The men of the castle dress Greta in Imipolex G and use her sexually (to her delight). She becomes Kundry, whom Klingsor enslaved and made to seduce knights. Erdmann, however, actually enjoys the role of Imipolex G guinea pig. She loses track of time until: "One morning I was outside the factory, naked, in the rain. Nothing grew there. Something had been deposited in a great fan that went on for miles. Some tarry kind of waste" (p. 488). This episode is juxtaposed with a scene in which Greta and her husband, Thanatz, wander hand in hand through the pine woods near a rocket site on the Lüneburg Heath (Blicero has adopted them to replace his previous Hänsel and Gretel, Katje and the soon-to-be-murdered Gottfried; thus Greta is referred to as Gretel in this passage). Again there are echoes of quest legend. They encounter a forbidding presence, which interdicts their explorations, but not before they recognize that they are in "the ruin of a great city, not an ancient ruin, but brought down in their lifetime" (p. 485). Both of these scenes depend for their effectiveness on associations with the magic destruction of the fortresses of evil sorcerers in grail-quest literature. When, for example, Parsifal resists the temptations of Kundry in Wagner's opera, Klingsor's castle and all his retinue simply disappear.

Pynchon uses grail-quest parallels judiciously. Neither of the two scenes described above really strains our credulity. While Greta's waking up "naked and alone" outside the castle is the usual transitional device in grail legend transformation scenes, the castle still stands, and ruined cities like the one Greta and Thanatz discover were common enough in 1945. Striking a sympathetic resonance in readers acquainted with the grail legends, Pynchon achieves an effect without sacrificing plausibility.

The strengths of Pynchon's method emerge in a comparison with another modern writer who makes use of the quest tradition, J. R. R. Tolkien. Written between 1936 and 1949, *The Lord of the Rings* is as much about World War II—allegorically—as is *Gravity's Rainbow*. Having actually experienced the war, however, Tolkien wrote a tale in which good and evil are so clearly defined as to have little bearing on the real, postwar world. From his later vantage in history, Pynchon can see that the clarity about good and evil during the war may have been one of its most dangerous legacies. Postwar man began zealously to dichotomize, especially along political lines, pathetically convinced that the difference between good and evil could still be made clear-cut. Tolkien, then, under the stimulus of his time, was a literary anomaly, a romancer. But Pynchon, too, is in many ways a romancer; his mythologizing is no less eclectic than that of Tolkien, and the elements of his fictions are in many ways more fabulous. The difference is that the romance of Pynchon's literature of possibilities is made plausible (and plausibility is the Achilles heel of all kinds of romance, from fairy tales to science fiction) by his thoroughgoing understanding of and grounding in the physical sciences. Pynchon uses science—which we usually think of as supporting a "common-sense" view of things—as a license for fantasy. Chastened, perhaps, by phenomena like the "particle zoo"—the proliferation of sub-atomic particles—he draws the obvious conclusion: that the complexity and multiplicity of reality are so great that for all our experience, all our reasoning, all our science, we are still, with Sir Isaac Newton, playing on the beach, the great ocean of truth all undiscovered before us.

But we know by now that science is the junior partner in Pynchon's fiction-making enterprise. Pynchon had the opportunity long ago to be a physicist, but he chose to be a humanist. The insights that science furnishes take on their greatest cogency when they are made relevant to man's aesthetic imagination—because where science, since Galileo, tends to humble man (while placating him with discrete quanta of delusory power over his environment), the arts exalt him. Thus Pynchon is a synthesizer, making science serve his aesthetic vision.

T. S. Eliot said that the individual literary talent both assimilates and modifies the literary tradition, and Pynchon does not violate this dictum. He assimilates and modifies both the "modern" tradition and the more venerable quest tradition, and he owes much to the document in which the one was sired on the other—Eliot's *The Waste Land*. Where the quest in Eliot's poem was highly ambiguous, the quests in Pynchon's books are conceded from the outset to be factitious and unresolvable. The quest was hard enough in the old literature, because only certain preternaturally pure knights could even come close to the ideal. Now it is harder yet, since we have lost not merely the object which an omnipotent being has endowed with special powers of spiritual healing, but also the very ground of certainty, the indispensable faith that made all kinds of quests worthwhile—and made reading about them edifying. Nor can we even say that we now quest for godhead itself rather than for the intermediary holy relic. It is a bleaker thing we undertake: we merely seek data about the real, while the goal—a little genuine understanding of the cosmos (certainly not mastery)—recedes before us with the discovery of each new subatomic particle. It is in grappling with our loss that a modern, agnostic literary tradition has emerged, and this, too, Pynchon has modified by showing us that uncertainty has its positive aspect. It is somehow reassuring to be confronted afresh with evidence of mystery. Pynchon has it both ways, celebrating the promise of the unknown without blinking the horrors of the Void. He shows us modern fragmentation and the uncertainty that bedevils science, with its constitutional need for precision, at the same time that he reassures us that worlds of unplumbed reality hold infinite promise. And like that other former student at Cornell, Oedipa Maas—whose age and domicile also coincide with his own—Thomas Pynchon finds worlds intersecting less in equations than in language.

Notes
Selected Bibliography
Index

Notes

1. Pynchon's Artistic Priorities

1. Letter to the author, 11 August 1975.
2. Letter to the author, 28 July 1975.
3. According to Mathew Winston, Pynchon had entered Cornell at the age of sixteen, having graduated in 1953 from Oyster Bay High School in Oyster Bay, Long Island. The recipient of an award for "the senior attaining the highest average in the study of English," Pynchon was also class salutatorian. "The Quest for Pynchon," *Twentieth Century Literature*, 21 (October 1975), 282.
4. These and subsequent recollections of Professor Bolton come from a conversation I had with him on 4 March 1976.
5. Quoted in Thomas Pynchon, *Gravity's Rainbow* (New York: Viking, 1973), p. 1. Subsequent page references will appear parenthetically in the text.
6. "The Most Irresponsible Bastard," *New Republic*, 14 April 1973, p. 24.
7. John A. Meixner, "The All-Purpose Quest," *Kenyon Review*, 25 (Autumn 1963), 729–35.
8. "Keeping Cool," *Commentary*, 36 (September 1963), 259.
9. *Commentary*, 56 (September 1973), 68.
10. Introduction, *Pynchon: A Collection of Critical Essays* (Englewood Cliffs, New Jersey: Prentice-Hall, 1978), p. 15.
11. *Critique*, 18, No. 3 (1977), 34.
12. "V. and V-2," *London Magazine*, NS 13 (February-March 1974), 84.
13. Representative articles include: Don Hausdorff, "Thomas Pynchon's Multiple Absurdities," *Wisconsin Studies in Contemporary Literature*, 7 (1966), 258–69; Roger B. Henkle, "Pynchon's Tapestries on the Western Wall," *Modern Fiction Studies*, 17 (1971), 207–20; and Joseph Fahy, "Thomas Pynchon's *V.* and Mythology," *Critique*, 18, No. 3 (1977), 5–18.
14. One of the best of these is Anne Mangel, "Maxwell's Demon, Entropy, Information: *The Crying of Lot 49*," *Tri-Quarterly*, 20 (Winter 1971), 194–208. See also Charles B. Harris, "Thomas Pynchon and the Entropic Vision," in *Contemporary American Novelists of the Absurd* (New Haven: College and University Press, 1971), pp. 76–99, and Peter L. Abernethy, "Entropy in Pynchon's *The Crying of Lot 49*," *Critique*, 14, No. 2 (1972), 18–33. The most exhaustive study of the theme of entropy in Pynchon to date is William Plater, *The Grim Phoenix: Reconstructing Thomas Pynchon* (Bloomington: Indiana University Press, 1978).
15. The best of these is Donald J. Greiner, "Fiction as History, History as Fiction: The Reader and Thomas Pynchon's *V.*," *South Carolina Review*, 10, No. 1 (1977), 4–18. See also Scott Sanders, "Pynchon's Paranoid History," *Twentieth Century Literature*, 21 (May 1975), 177–92.

16. "Pentecost, Promiscuity, and Pynchon's *V.:* From the Scaffold to the Impulsive," *Twentieth Century Literature,* 21 (May 1975), 163–76.
17. *Pynchon: Creative Paranoia in "Gravity's Rainbow"* (Port Washington, New York: Kennikat, 1978), p. 4.
18. Thomas Pynchon, *V.* (Philadelphia and New York: Lippincott, 1963), p. 80. Subsequent page references will appear parenthetically in the text.
19. *Thomas Pynchon* (New York: Warner Paperback Library, 1974), pp. 21–32.
20. Pynchon is probably aware that *Stollen* are also sections—bars—of a minnesinger's song.
21. *Thomas Pynchon,* p. 45.

2. Surface and Void

1. On the dominance of the Terrible Mother in the collective unconscious of contemporary America, see Harold Schechter, "Kali on Main Street: The Rise of the Terrible Mother in America," *Journal of Popular Culture,* 7 (Fall 1973), 251–63. Schechter documents the preeminence of this archetype in the seventies, tracing the warning signals back to the proceding decade. He might well have included *V.,* published in 1963.
2. Walter Pater, *Studies in the History of the Renaissance* (London: Macmillan, 1873), pp. 45, 49.
3. "Pynchon's Tapestries on the Western Wall," *Modern Fiction Studies,* 17 (1971), 209.
4. *The White Goddess,* 3rd ed. amended and enlarged (London: Faber, 1952), p. 393.
5. Rainer Maria Rilke's poem *"Die Geburt des Venus"* concludes, after the goddess steps ashore, with the washing-up of a dead dolphin, *"tod, rot, und offen."*
6. It is interesting to note the reference to "pack ice" in Robert Graves's "The White Goddess" (the poem, not the book).
7. Note the similarly named Sons of the Red Apocalypse in "Lowlands."
8. Thomas Pynchon, *The Crying of Lot 49* (Philadelphia and New York: Lippincott, 1966), p. 170. Subsequent page references will appear parenthetically in the text.
9. This would have been the exhibition remembered by Oedipa. She could not have seen the completed triptych earlier than 1962, as the last panel was not finished until that year. The triptych would have been exhibited again in 1964, but that is "present time" in the novel—too late for Oedipa's flashback. Of course this kind of strict chronology was probably never intended. Pynchon doubtless sent Pierce and Oedipa to the same exhibit (or to a composite of the exhibits) he himself had attended.
10. See, for example, Octavio Paz and Roger Caillois, eds., *Remedios Varo* (Mexico City, D.[istrito] F.[ederal], 1966). This book includes articles, comments, and notes by Octavio Paz, Roger Caillois, Juliana Gonzalez, Walter Gruen, and the artist herself. In subsequent references to this book, translations from the Spanish are my own.
11. Ibid., p. 165.
12. Benjamin Peret was part of a circle that included André Breton, Paul Eluard, Max Ernst, Yves Tanguy, and Joan Miró. The intellectual cross-fertilization was doubtless of major importance in the development of Varo's mature style. Ida

Rodriguez Prampolini, *El Surrealismo y el Arte Fantastico de Mexico* (Mexico City: Universidad Autonoma de Mexico Instituto de Investigaciones Esteticas, 1969), discusses Varo's work in the light of ideas and pronouncements of the preeminent surrealist theoreticians.

13. Paz and Caillois, *Remedios Varo*, p. 178.

14. Ibid., p. 166.

3. "Making the Unreal Reel"

1. Marshall McLuhan, *Understanding Media* (New York: McGraw-Hill, 1964), p. 284.

2. Mathew Winston, "The Quest for Pynchon," *Twentieth Century Literature*, 21 (October 1975), 284.

3. *From Caligari to Hitler: A Psychological Study of the German Film* (Princeton: Princeton University Press, 1947), p. 320. For a fuller discussion of Pynchon's allusions to German film and his use of Kracauer, see my "Cinematic Auguries of the Third Reich in *Gravity's Rainbow*," *Literature/Film Quarterly*, 6 (October 1978), 364–70.

4. As we see in his article on the aftermath of the riots in the Watts section of Los Angeles, "A Journey into the Mind of Watts," *The New York Times Magazine*, 12 June 1966, pp. 34–35, 78, 80–82, 84.

5. Gottfried is in a sense the brother of Ilse Pökler. *Lohengrin's* Gottfried turns out to be the brother of the similarly named heroine, Elsa. The bridal imagery of the book's conclusion may also derive from *Lohengrin*.

6. I am indebted in what follows to an unpublished analysis of the movie by Eric Hyman.

7. *Anatomy of Criticism* (Princeton: Princeton University Press, 1957), p. 288.

8. *Feeling and Form* (New York: Scribners, 1953), p. 412.

9. "Rocket Power," *Saturday Review of the Arts*, 1 (March 1973), 60.

10. Ernst Klee and Otto Merk, *The Birth of the Missile*, trans. T. Schoeters (New York: Dutton, 1965), p. 12.

11. The Germans really did have a rocket called the *Enzian*. It was an antiaircraft version of the A4, according to Klee and Merk, pp. 68, 86–87. Development of German antiaircraft weapons was carried out under Project Fire Lily, a name that figures in the South-West African chapter of *V.*, in which Mondaugen and Weissmann were first introduced. Did *Gravity's Rainbow* grow out of material left over from *V.*?

12. Vol. V of *The Standard Edition of the Complete Psychological Works of Sigmund Freud*, trans. James Strachey (London: Hogarth, 1958), p. 410.

13. This is not just any wrecked automobile. It is a wrecked Hannomag Storm, with one door standing open—which means it is the one in whose crash Wernher von Braun broke his arm March 16, 1945. He had been traveling from Bleicheröde to Berlin at night (to avoid strafing by American planes) when his chauffeur dozed off and lost control of the car. Though badly hurt in the ensuing crash, von Braun managed to shoulder the door open and drag the unconscious driver out of the wreck before it caught fire and he blacked out. Pynchon casually refers to von Braun's "wrecked arm in a plaster cast" (p. 237) much earlier in the book. The author could have taken these details from James McGovern's *Crossbow and Overcast* (New York: Morrow, 1964), p. 94.

14. "Antipointsman/Antimexico: Some Mathematical Imagery in *Gravity's Rainbow,*" *Critique,* 16 (1974), 73–90.

15. Smithfield Market was the site of a particularly costly V-2 hit late in the war, as we learn from an important Pynchon source: David Irving's *The Mare's Nest* (Boston: Little, Brown, 1965), p. 240.

16. Pynchon's details here come from Walter Dornberger's *V-2,* trans. James Cleugh and Geoffrey Halliday (New York: Viking, 1954), p. 57. General Dornberger commanded the Peenemünde Rocket Research Institute during the war.

17. Quoted in David Robinson, *The History of World Cinema* (London: Eyre-Methuen, 1973), p. 60.

18. Ibid., p. 129.

19. *The Poetry of Ezra Pound* (Norfolk, Connecticut: New Directions, 1951), p. 262.

20. Sergei Eisenstein, *The Film Sense,* ed. and trans. Jay Leyda (London: Faber, 1943), p. 14.

21. Sergei Eisenstein, *Film Form* (New York: Harcourt, Brace, 1949), pp. 60–61.

22. Kenner, *Ezra Pound,* p. 261.

23. Eisenstein, *Film Form,* p. 38.

4. *"Unthinkable Order": Music in Pynchon*

1. Letter to the author, 25 March 1976.

2. *Epoch,* 9 (Spring 1959), 201. Subsequent page references will appear parenthetically in the text.

3. But see William Vesterman, "Pynchon's Poetry," *Twentieth Century Literature,* 21, (May 1975), 211–20.

4. "Pynchon's Gravity," *New Review,* 3, No. 27 (1976), 39.

5. *The Noble Savage,* No. 3 (1961), p. 224. Subsequent page references will appear parenthetically in the text.

6. According to the *Oxford English Dictionary,* "moldweorp" ("earth-thrower") is Old English for mole; however, versions of the word have survived in British dialect into the present. One of the quotations in the O.E.D. is from a little-known Jacobean play, *Tryall of Cheualry* (III.i): "I took you for a spy. Yet saw me not no more than a molewarp." The word also occurs in Shakespeare, as does 'porpentine' (porcupine). Just as spies operate inconspicuously—"under the rose"—these creatures of the field are seldom seen. Moldweorp and his crew, one of whom first appears wearing a hawk's head mask, are a threat to the defenseless Wrens (and the frail civilization behind them). The maladroit porcupine must try to save the Wrens. Empire at the animal level reminds one of "Her Majesty's Servants," Kipling's tale of beasts of burden in the army.

7. An ironic version of Victoria's entreaty will be played when Carla Maijstral begs Sidney Stencil to protect her husband, whose life is in jeopardy because he is working for the British, spying on V. and her pro-Italian activities on Malta. The Maijstrals's granddaughter, Paola, will like Manon and Victoria become both an exile and a prostitute.

8. Robert Craft, "Nijinsky and 'Le Sacre,' " *New York Review of Books,* 15 April 1976, p. 36.

9. Igor Stravinsky, *An Autobiography* (New York: Norton, 1962), p. 31.
10. Ibid.
11. *Music in the Twentieth Century* (New York: Norton, 1966), pp. 380, 381.

5. Intersecting Worlds: Language and Literature

1. "The Quest for Pynchon," *Twentieth Century Literature*, 21 (October 1975), 284.
2. Mr. Bailey shared his recollections with me in a telephone conversation on 2 June 1976.
3. Bailey says that his brother-in-law, William B. Clarke, once received a letter from Pynchon in which he commented brilliantly on a number of points in a technical article written by Clarke for one of Boeing's publications.
4. Introduction, *Selected Writings of Edgar Allan Poe* (Boston: Houghton Mifflin, 1956), p. xxi.
5. *The Narrative of Arthur Gordon Pym of Nantucket*, Vol. III of *The Complete Works of Edgar Allan Poe*, ed. James A. Harrison (New York: Crowell, 1902), p. 242.
6. *John Webster's Borrowing* (Berkeley and Los Angeles: University of California Press, 1960), p. 161.
7. *The Literature of the English Renaissance 1485—1660 (New York: Collier, 1969), p. 173.*
8. *Introduction, Three Jacobean Tragedies* (Harmondsworth, Middlesex: Penguin Books, 1965), p. 28.
9. Ibid., pp. 17–18.
10. *Life Against Death: The Psychooanalytic Meaning of History* (Middletown, Connecticut: Wesleyan University Press, 1959), p. ix.
11. Richard Fariña, *Long Time Coming and A Long Time Gone* (New York: Random House, 1969), p. 138.
12. Ibid., p. 12.
13. ' "The Goddess and the Schlemihl," *The New Leader*, 18 March 1963, p. 23.
14. *The Collected Tales of E. M. Forster* (New York: Alfred A. Knopf, 1952), p. 252.
15. Introduction, *Two Stories and a Memory*, by Giuseppe di Lampedusa (London: Collins and Harvill Press, 1962), p. 15.
16. C. F. MacIntyre, trans. *Duino Elegies*, by Rainer Maria Rilke (Berkeley: University of California Press, 1963), p. xi.
17. Jung describes a number of dreams in which there is movement to the left or right around a mandalic circle in his "Individual Dream Symbolism in Relation to Alchemy," in *Psychology and Alchemy*, Vol. XII of *The Collected Works of C. G. Jung*, trans. R. F. C. Hull, 2nd ed., Bollingen Series XX (Princeton: Princeton University Press, 1968). See also M. L. von Franz, "The Process of Individuation," in *Man and His Symbols*, ed. Carl Gustav Jung (Jew York: Doubleday, 1964), p. 215.
18. *Anatomy of Criticism*, p. 146.
19. It should be *Die Leid-Stadt*, but Pynchon is remembering the genitive construction used in the poem: *"wie fremd sind die Gassen der Leid-Stadt"* (how strange are the streets of the City of Pain). We might explain this as a mistake on the part of that tiresome know-it-all, Mr. Information (who makes the Happyville/*Leid-Stadt* comparison), if Pynchon did not make similar mistakes elsewhere, e.g., *Der Meistersinger* (p. 361), *terre mauvais* (p. 69), *Un Perm au Casino Hermann Goering (perm* is short for *permission*—a furlough—which is feminine).

20. Robert Coover, "Dedicatorio y Prólogo a Don Miguel de Cervantes Saavedra," to "Seven Exemplary Fictions" in *Pricksongs and Descants* (New York: Dutton, 1969), p. 77.

Selected Bibliography

Works by Thomas Pynchon

"The Small Rain." *Cornell Writer*, 6 (March 1959), 14–32.
"Mortality and Mercy in Vienna." *Epoch*, 9 (Spring 1959), 195–213.
"Low-lands." *New World Writing*, 16 (1960), 85–108.
"Entropy." *Kenyon Review*, 22 (Spring 1960), 277–92.
"Under the Rose." *Noble Savage*, 3 (May 1961), 113–51.
V. Philadelphia and New York: J. B. Lippincott, 1963.
"The Secret Integration." *Saturday Evening Post*, 237 (December 19, 1964), 36, 39, 42–44, 46–49, 51.
"The World (This One), the Flesh (Mrs. Oedipa Maas), and the Testament of Pierce Inverarity." *Esquire*, 44 (December 1965), 164–65.
"The Shrink Flips." *Cavalier*, 16 (March 1966), 32–33, 88–92.
The Crying of Lot 49. Philadelphia and New York: J. B. Lippincott, 1966.
"A Journey into the Mind of Watts." *New York Times Magazine*, June 12, 1966, pp. 34–35, 78, 80–82, 84.
Gravity's Rainbow. New York: Viking, 1973.

Criticism and Bibliography

Cowart, David. "Cinematic Auguries of the Third Reich in *Gravity's Rainbow*." *Literature/Film Quarterly*, 6 (October 1978), 364–70.
———. "Pynchon's Use of the Tannhäuser-Legend in Gravity's Rainbow." *Notes on Contemporary Literature*, 9 (May 1979), 2–3.
Friedman, Alan, and Manfred Puetz. "Science as Metaphor: Thomas Pynchon's *Gravity's Rainbow*." *Contemporary Literature*, 15 (1974), 345–59.
Greiner, Donald J. "Fiction as History, History as Fiction: The Reader and Thomas Pynchon's *V.*" *South Carolina Review*, 10 (November 1977), 4–18.
Harris, Charles B. "Thomas Pynchon and the Entropic Vision." In his *Contemporary American Novelists of the Absurd.* New Haven: College and University Press, 1971.
Herzberg, Bruce. "Selected Articles on Thomas Pynchon: An Annotated Bibliography." *Twentieth Century Literature*, 21 (May 1975), 221–25.
Hyman, Stanley Edgar. "The Goddess and the Schlemihl." *The New Leader*, March 18, 1963, pp. 22–23.
Kolodny, Annette, and Daniel Peters. "Pynchon's *The Crying of Lot 49:* The Novel as Subversive Experience." *Modern Fiction Studies*, 19 (Spring 1973), 79–87.
Krafft, John. "And How Far-Fallen: Puritan Themes in *Gravity's Rainbow*." *Critique*, 18 (1977), 55–73.

143

144 Selected Bibliography

Leverenz, David, and George Levine, eds. *Mindful Pleasures: Essays on Thomas Pynchon.* Boston: Little, Brown, 1976.
Lhamon, W. T., Jr. "The Most Irresponsible Bastard." *New Republic,* April 14, 1973, pp. 24–28.
McConnell, Frank D. *Four Postwar American Novelists: Bellow, Mailer, Barth, and Pynchon.* Chicago: University of Chicago Press, 1977.
———. "Thomas Pynchon." In *Contemporary Novelists.* Ed. James Vinson. London: St. James Press, 1972, pp. 1033–36.
Mendelson, Edward. *Pynchon: A Collection of Critical Essays.* Englewood Cliffs, New Jersey: Prentice-Hall, 1978.
———. "Pynchon's Gravity." *Yale Review,* 62 (Summer 1963), 624–31.
———. "Rainbow Corner." *Times Literary Supplement,* June 13, 1975, p. 666.
Ozier, Lance. "Antipointsman/Antimexico: Some Mathematical Imagery in *Gravity's Rainbow.*" *Critique,* 16 (1974), 73–90.
———. "The Calculus of Transformation: More Mathematical Imagery in *Gravity's Rainbow.*" *Twentieth Century Literature,* 21 (May 1975), 193–210.
Plater, William M. *The Grim Phoenix: Reconstructing Thomas Pynchon.* Bloomington: Indiana University Press, 1978.
Poirier, Richard. "Cook's Tour." *New York Review of Books,* 1 (1963), 32.
———. "Embattled Underground" *New York Times Book Review,* May 1, 1966, pp. 5, 42–43.
Siegel, Mark Richard. *Pynchon: Creative Paranoia in "Gravity's Rainbow."* Port Washington, New York: Kennikat, 1978.
Simmon, Scott. "A Character Index: *Gravity's Rainbow.*" *Critique,* 16 (1974), 68–72.
———. "*Gravity's Rainbow* Described." *Critique,* 16 (1974), 54–67.
Slade, Joseph W. "Escaping Rationalization: Options for the Self in *Gravity's Rainbow.*" *Critique,* 18 (1977), 27–38.
———. *Thomas Pynchon.* New York: Warner Paperback Library, 1974.
Weixlmann, Joseph. "Thomas Pynchon: A Bibliography." *Critique,* 14 (1972), 34–43.
Wolfley, Lawrence C. "Repression's Rainbow: The Presence of Norman O. Brown in Pynchon's Big Novel." *PMLA,* 92 (October 1977), 873–89.

Index

Santayana, George, 97
Sarajevo, Yugoslavia, 66
Satin, 75, 77
Saturday Review, 6
Schlabone, Gustav: argument with Säure
    about music, 82–88 passim; plays
    Haydn Kazoo Quartet, 90
Schlepzig, Max: in *Alpdrücken*, 39; in
    Jugend Herauf!, 53; Slothrop
    impersonates, 34, 355
Schönberg, Arnold, 12, 78, 90
Schwarzbach, F. S., 65
Schwarzgerät, 43, 129
Schwarzknabe, 43, 46
Schwarzkommando: "generated" by film,
    37–38, 40, 45, 46, 49; and KEZVH
    insignia, 122–23; leadership, 47, 49;
    "old Tribal unity," 122–23, 130; Slo-
    throp aids, 129
Schwarzvater, 43
Selma, Alabama, 5
Serialism. *See* twelve-tone music
Sgherraccio, 18
Shadow, The: links *The Crying of Lot 49*
    and *Gravity's Rainbow*, 89–90
Shakespeare, William: *Hamlet*, 102, 103;
    Titus Andronicus, 103; mentioned, 3,
    97, 110, 140*n*6
Shekhinah, 53
Sieg im Western, 37, 38
Siegel, Cleanth, 64–65, 78
Siegel, Mark, 8
Sklar, Robert, 6
Slab, 106
Slade, Joseph, critical work on Pynchon
    by, 7, 10, 12, 98
Slothrop, Broderick, 50
Slothrop, Tyrone: in the Abreaction
    Ward, 37, 41, 50, 80; as Christ figure,
    47–48; dreams of, 49, 50–54; his dis-
    guises, 129; qua Fay Wray, 42, 47; qua
    Fisher King, 49; qua Max Schlepzig,
    34–35; qua Orpheus, 47, 87–88, 92;
    qua questing knight, 12930; qua Shir-
    ley Temple, 50, 52; "uncentered,"
    123–24; mentioned, 32–62 passim, 84,
    85, 100, 112, 113, 121, 122, 125–26,
    127
Slothrop, William, 60
Smith, Sir Denis Nayland, 58
Smithfield Market, hit by V-2, 55, 55*n*
Snake, 52
Sound, physical properties of, 87–88

Sound-shadow, 89–90, 92, 94
South Pole. *See* Antarctic
South-West Africa: Dodgsonian "mirror
    time" and, 112; Foppl's siege party in,
    21; Germans in, 16, 51, 122; 139*n11*;
    legendary connection with Argentina
    and, 40–41; Weissmann in, 120
Spade, Sam, 127
Sparagmos, Slothrop's fate as, 47
Special Operations Executive, Pirate
    Prentice leaves, 55, 56
Sphere, McClintick, identified as Or-
    nette Coleman, 114
Spohr, Ludwig, 88
Spontini, Gasparo Luigi Pacifico, 88
Springer. *See* Göll, Gerhardt von
Squalidozzi, Francisco, 40, 53, 129
Squarcione, Rocco, 11
Squasimodeo, 79
Stencil, Herbert: dates metamorphosis
    of Victoria Wren into V., 18, 19;
    paranoia of, 13; quest of, 32, 67, 100,
    127, 128; as son of V., 14; unreliability
    of, 19, 73
Stencil, Sidney, 76, 101, 140*n7*
Stockhausen, Karlheinz, 9, 65, 78, 81, 82
Stoker, Bram, 97
Stravinsky, Igor: *Le Chant du Rossignol*,
    75; qua Vladimir Porcépic; and *Rite of
    Spring* compared with *L'Enlèvement des
    Vierges Chinoises*, 74–75; *Rite of Spring*,
    65, 78, 115; mentioned, 12
Submariner. *See* Comic books
Superman, 58, 60. *See also* Comic books
Swift, Jonathan, 108
Symmes, John Cleves, 101

Tagliacozzi, 12
Takeshi and Ichizo, 51
Tallis, Thomas, 12
Tanguy, Yves, 138*n12*
Tanner, Tony, 6, 7
Tannhäuser, 12, 129. *See also* Wagner,
    Richard
Tarot, 124
Tchaikovsky, Peter Ilyich, 78
Tchitcherine, Vaslav, 35, 42, 52, 112,
    129
Temple, Shirley, 50, 52
Tenniel, Sir John, 113
Tennyson, Alfred Lord: "Locksley
    Hall," 122; mentioned, 97
Tetragrammaton, 124